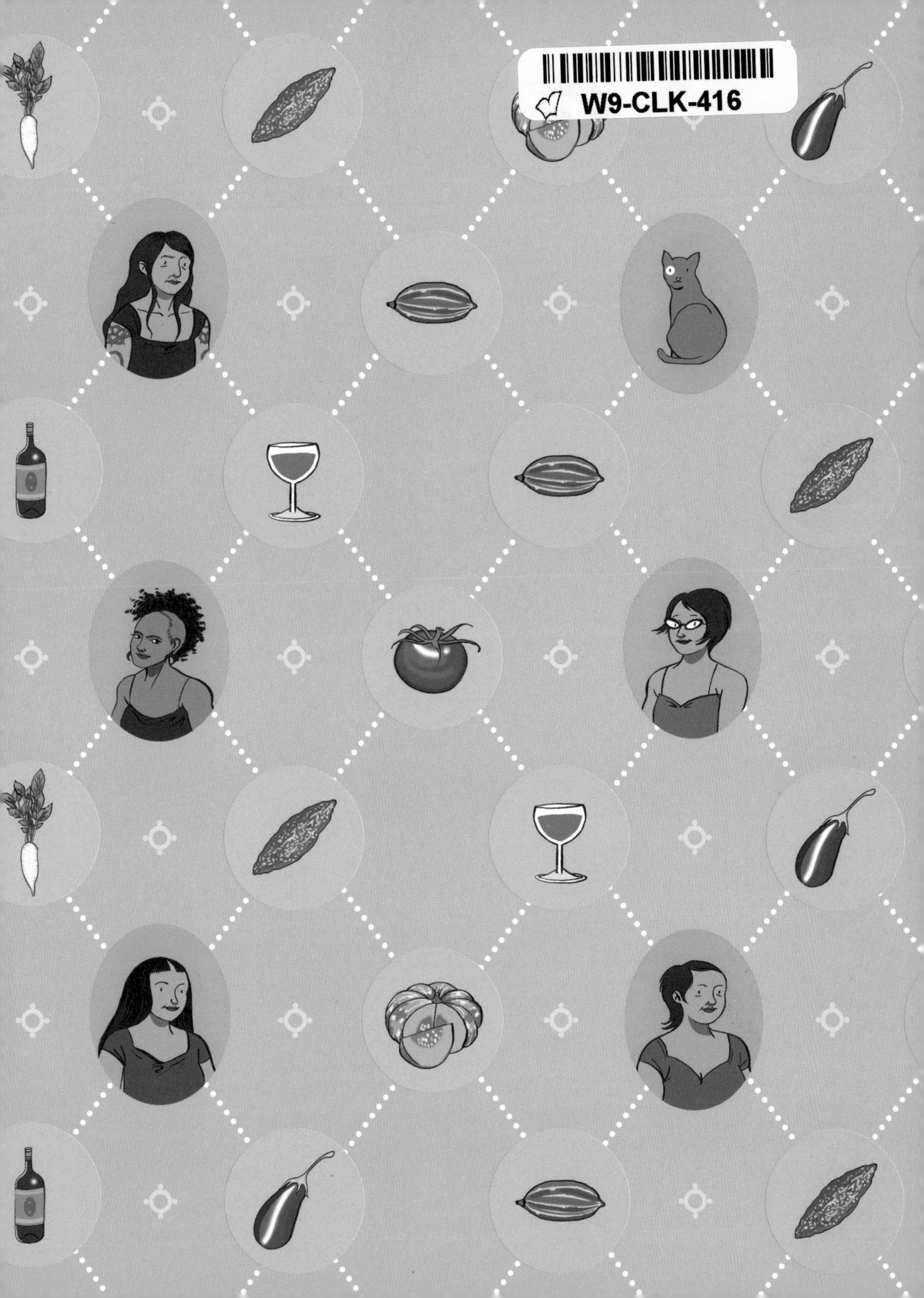

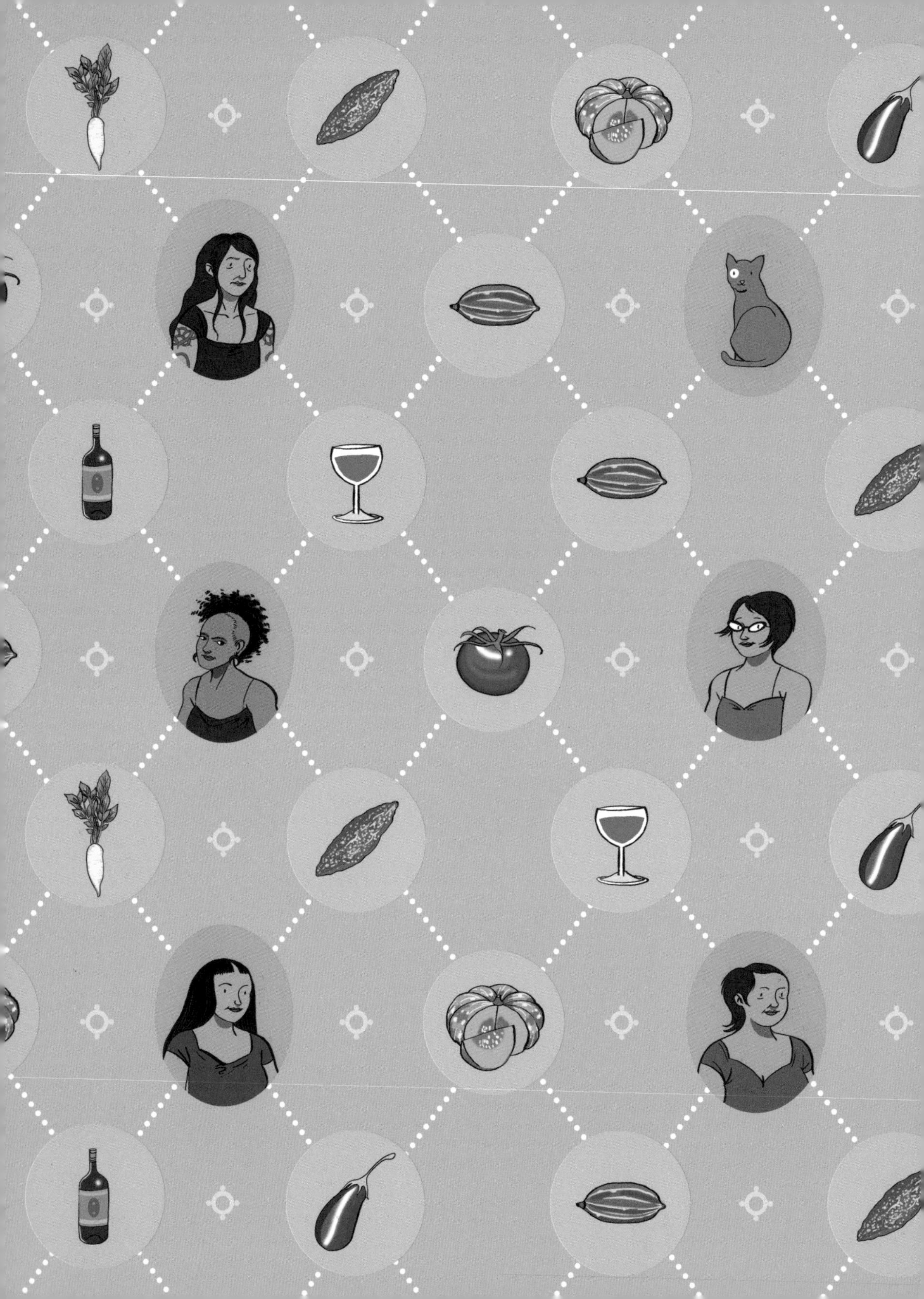

More Praise For *Spellbound*

"By turns melancholy and sensual, each beautifully-observed line in *Spellbound* drew me into the parallel lives of Bishakh and Anjali. An intoxicating love letter to grabbing the rudder of life and setting out for unknown waters."
—Hazel Newlevant, author of *No Ivy League*

"*Spellbound: A Graphic Memoir* flows like a beautiful conversation between two selves. Bishakh Som transcends chronicling lived experiences by breathing life into Anjali and giving her a reality of her own. In this imagined parallel reality, we are guided by honesty, longing, and curiosity to a greater understanding of Som's trans journey. I am especially compelled by the depiction of navigating interpersonal relationships while coming to a fuller understanding of the self. Som has documented this process with the utmost sincerity and imaginative wit!"
—JR Zuckerberg author of *A Quick and Easy Guide to Queer & Trans Identities*

"*Spellbound* is an engrossing read, examining complicated relationships—family, friendships, and romances alike—with natural, intuitive, and carefully-observed craft. Bishakh Som's work throughout is thoughtful, witty, and beautifully inked—a delightful read from start to finish."
—Melanie Gillman, author of *As the Crow Flies* and *Stage Dreams*

"Bishakh Som discovers the power and potential in creating an alter-ego who both is, and is not, the self in this gorgeously drawn almost-memoir. Using the character of Anjali, Som writes about an international childhood spent in Ethiopia, India, and New York City. She writes of the death of her parents and the gutsy decision to quit a dull, safe job to pursue an uncertain creative dream. We, the readers, are the benefactors of this leap into the unknown. How fortunate that Anjali, and Som, chose comics!" —Maia Kobabe, author of *Gender Queer: A Memoir*

"Bishakh Som's *Spellbound* is the delightful, moving, engrossing story of the child of immigrants who does her best to fulfil her parents' ambitions for her, before realizing that she has her own very different life to live. Beautifully told through the details of everyday life, *Spellbound* shows how we may have to learn a little of the art of living before we will know how to make art, and that if the truth of our life is being transgender, it is never too late — or too early — to come out to oneself and the world."
— McKenzie Wark, author of *The Beach Beneath the Street*

BISHAKH SOM

Spellbound

a Graphic Memoir

STREET NOISE BOOKS • BROOKLYN, NEW YORK

Library of Congress CIP data available.

ISBN 978-1-951-491-03-1

Edited by Ada Price
Book design by Liz Frances

Printed in South Korea

9 8 7 6 5 4 3 2 1

First Edition

To my wife Joan, my brother Suj, Ollie the cat,
and to the memory of my sweet friend Tobias Tak — a beautiful soul
and an amazing, transcendent artist.

With thanks and love to Liz Frances, Ada Price, Patricia Fabricant,
and Adam McGovern.

Oh hey! I'm so psyched you could make it.

Have a seat! Did you get the Rioja? It's so good, right? Totally tastes like dill.

So I'm Bishakh — the author and illustrator of the juicy volume you're holding in your hot little hands. And I wanted to clue you in to what this book is all about.

1

So in 2012, I quit my full-time job in architecture to take a stab at writing and drawing a graphic novel — a collection of short stories. I had been drawing comics most of my life but never thought I could do it "seriously." When I eventually sent that first book to publishers and was waiting for responses, I began documenting my daily experiences.

I had been avoiding doing comics about myself on principle but I figured, who knows, maybe it'll be therapeutic. Loath to draw myself, however, I substituted Anjali, a cisgender Bengali-American woman in place of yours truly into these recollections.

I realize, in retrospect, that I had resorted to this substitution for another reason: because — well, 'cause Mademoiselle Anjali, c'est moi.

Or at least, she is who I thought I could be.

To unravel that last claim, let me take you back a little ways in time.

2

As a teen, desperate for some kind of identity to bring my blurry sense of self into focus, and being something of a moody child anyway, I dove head-first into the murky business of — brace yourselves — being a goth.

Press the Eject and Give me the Tape, by Bauhaus, Bleecker Bob's

Handmade mohair jumper, Camden Market

Tripp skinny black jeans, Enz's

Pointy leather buckled boots, Trash & Vaudeville

ENZ'S

I loved losing myself in black outfits, teasing my hair into a rat's nest, sporting Kohl-rimmed eyes.

Please cut your hair, beta... you look like a girl!

Needless to say, my parents were none too pleased with this unkempt, eccentric version of me.

And my "cohorts" at college mistook my subcultural identity for some-thing else :

Hey! You know what we used to call you on west campus?

Uh... no. Wh-what?

"Walking AIDS!" Haw haw!

What was I supposed to do? I wasn't a gay boy, but I didn't feel quite straight either. Everyone else had their own little niches: the queers, the jocks, the deadheads, the nerds. I didn't even really jibe with the few other goths on campus. Where did I fit in?

After grad school, I started to veer away from my goth trajectory. This is when I thought I should make a go of cultivating a career. I cut my hair into a sleek Vidal Sassoon bob and wore lots of J. Crew.

Bishakh is working at I.M. Pei's office! You know, they designed the Louvre museum? We are so proud of him!

OH GOD

Achchha?

All of which pleased my parents no end.

But as you'll soon find out, this arrangement didn't last very long. I was soon unmoored, alone, left to my own devices.

That's when things started to change.

Well, to say much more now might be overkill, but it was not so long after this that I started working on the comics you're about to read — when I invented Anjali as a second identity.

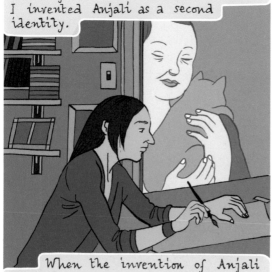

When the invention of Anjali started to mean something more.

So ... let's leave it at that for the moment, shall we? I'll go get another glass of this excellent Rioja. You go ahead and dive in.

Quit

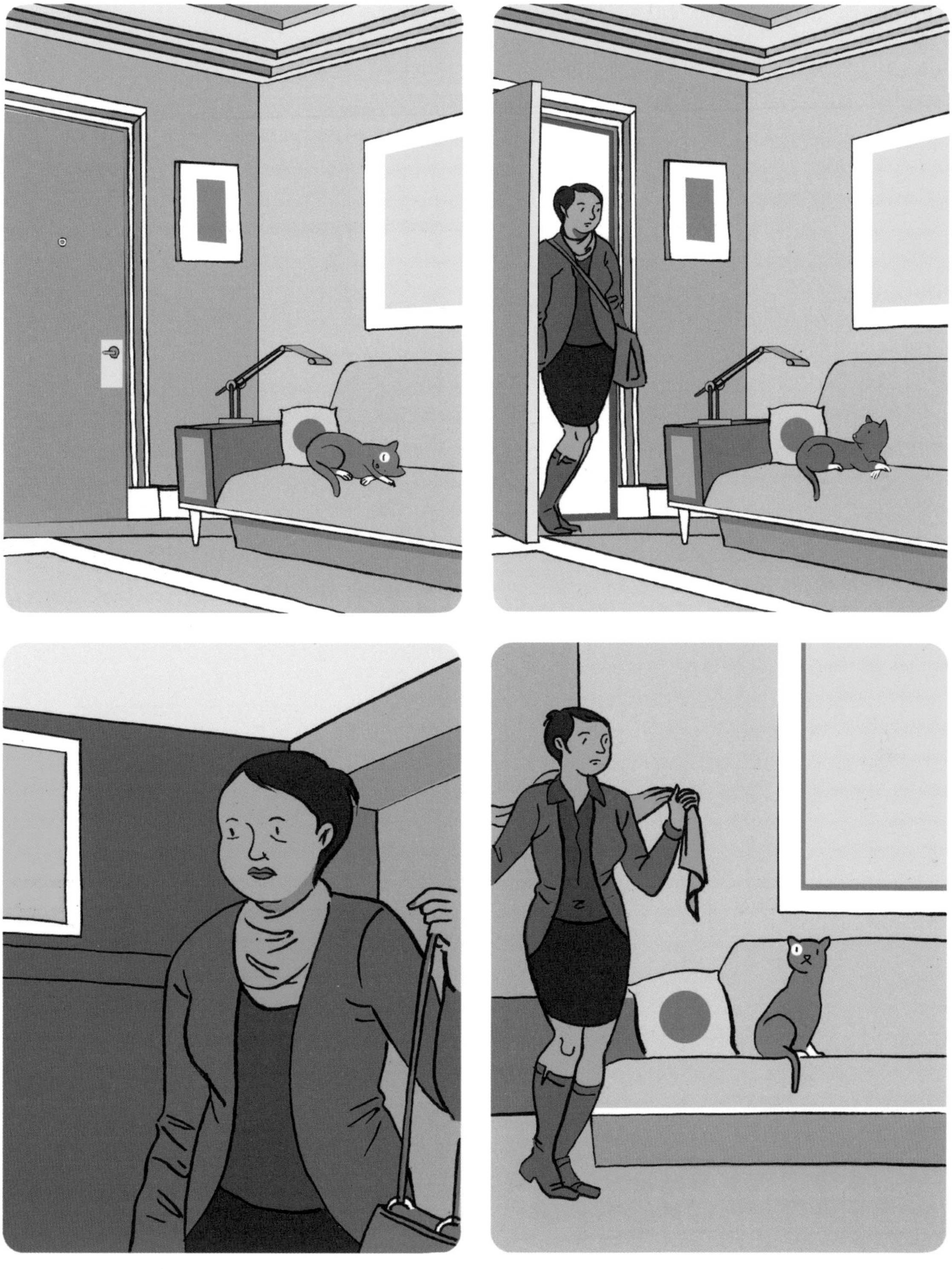

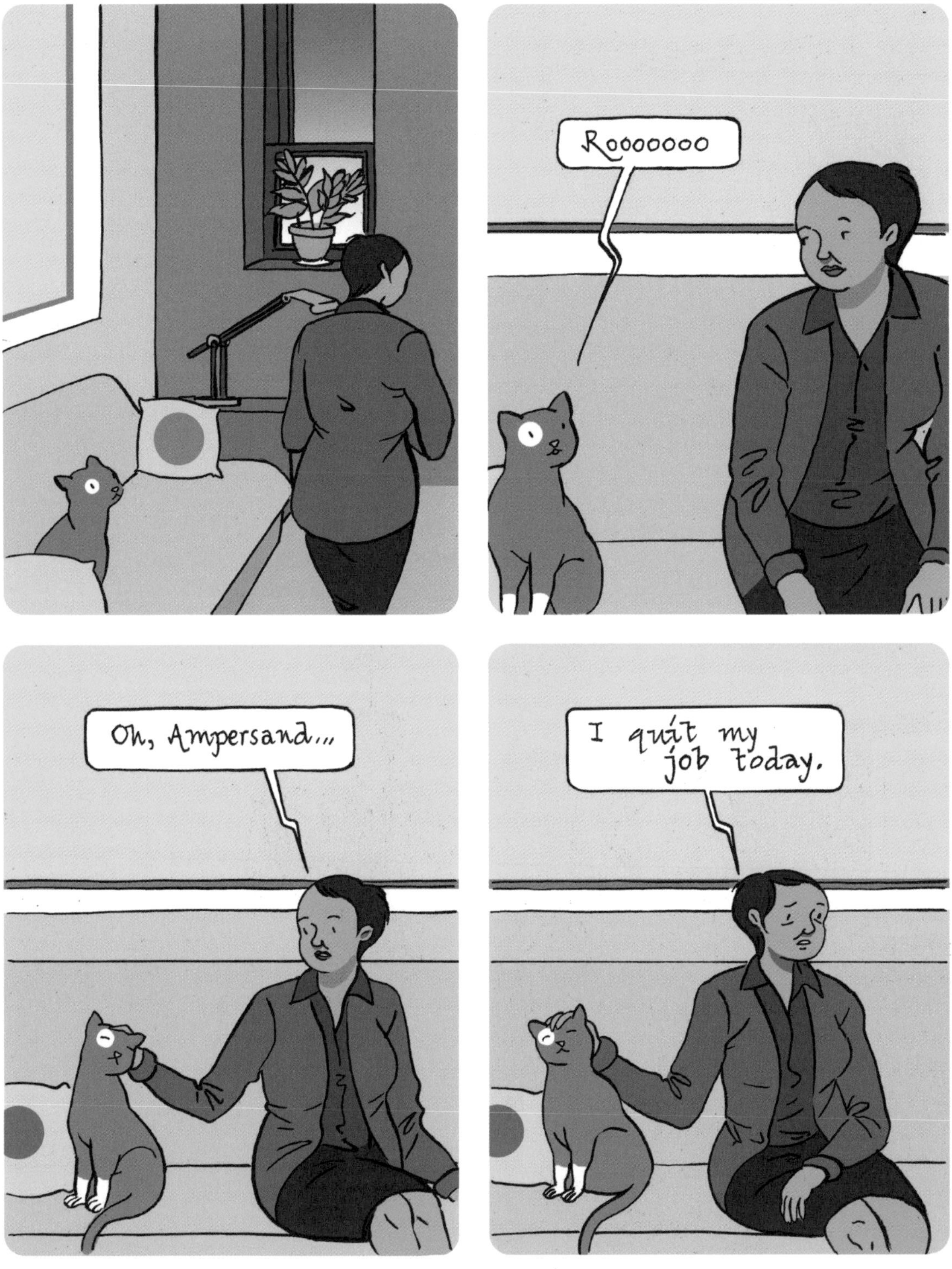
Rooooooo
Oh, Ampersand...
I quit my job today.

So then he says he's *cutting off* our health insurance! Just like that! And I'm like "What do you mean?" And he's like "Well, you're all young and healthy...you don't need to go to the doctor, do you?"

And I am aghast.
Absolutely dumbfounded.
So I said, "Are you crazy?! I need monthly medications!" And he was all "Oh, what do you take?" And I'm like "I'm not telling you that!"

And that was just the last straw. No paychecks for a month, weird-ass erratic behavior and then no health insurance? So I'm like, this is *insane*.
And I quit.

Oh my god.

I know.

7

The man doesn't even understand the *concept* of health insurance!

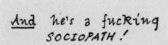

And <u>he's</u> a fucking *SOCIOPATH!*

GRRRRRR

OK, Miss Sharp, knives back in the knife drawer, please.

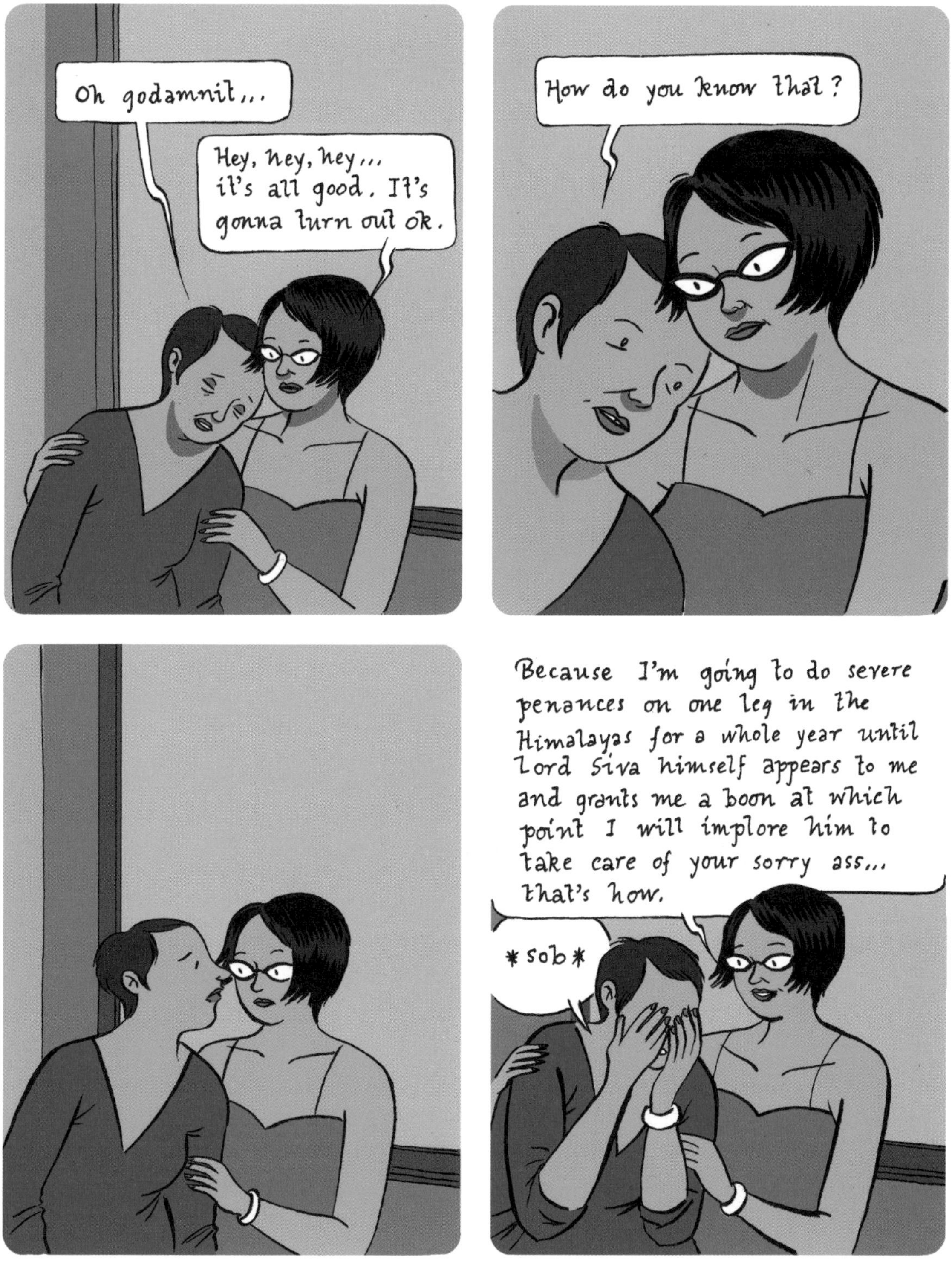
Oh godamnit...
Hey, hey, hey... it's all good. It's gonna turn out ok.
How do you know that?
Because I'm going to do severe penances on one leg in the Himalayas for a whole year until Lord Siva himself appears to me and grants me a boon at which point I will implore him to take care of your sorry ass... that's how.
sob

Maybe it was impetuous. But I just could *not* bear being in that office. The atmosphere was just *TOXIC.*

And you know, I'd been thinking about leaving anyway for a while. It just took one incident to give me the push I needed to actually do it.

What? I know... it's — it's foolish. But I felt like my life was coming to a crisis point. And — what?

Well, I — I have some savings from my dad's estate and my aunt left me some money, so I was thinking...

I — I was thinking I'd take a year off and — no, don't laugh — I thought I'd work on that graphic novel I was telling you about. I — I've got, like, 120 pages done already, so if I can get 80 more pages done, it'll make a nice book. And at the end of the year, I'll send it out to publishers and see if anyone bites.

I — I could do some freelance graphic design or illustration too... or architecture if I need to, but — who knows? I could — imagine it — actually do something I'm good at and that I like doing!

And — and if the book takes off, then — I don't know — it could be a whole new beginning! You know, I feel like everything — all the anxiety and craziness and *death* — it's all led up to this, to doing something meaningful — what?

Well, THANK YOU for the vote of CONFIDENCE!

roo roo

Day One of my new life post architecture. Feels weird to not be on the F train at this hour. Ampersand is thoroughly enjoying my late start to the day.

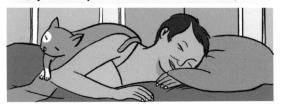

Day One also of austerity measures which means a cauliflower stalk, beet greens, broccoli stem, & potato curry for brunch.

Ampersand howls for his dinner starting at 3:00. I fend him off until 4:30. I wish I had a pair of noise-cancelling headphones.

6:30 rolls around and I've pencilled exactly... one page. But a very nice page it is.

A strong cup of PG Tips with milk and sugar — and I plunge into work. I can't believe it — 8 straight hours of drawing.

Fiddling around for a soundtrack to my new workday, I put on the BBC Asian Network and settle into a Bollywood coma.

A good day's work means I can treat myself to a leavings-free dinner, so, baked macaroni with tomatoes, capers, eggplant & caramelized onions.

Day two. Luckily I'd been doing thumbnails of this latest story on weekends and evenings while I was still at Chad's office, which means I can dive right into pencilling.

It's been so long since I sat down to work on art or comics and this time I'm gambling that a concerted effort will result in a momentous life-shift. It's still a little early to feel like a fraud but I'm sure that will come soon enough.

I've got one more page pencilled by 3pm and decide to take a well-deserved cleaning break, seeing as so much stuff has accumulated around my desk, mingling with dust bunnies, Ampersand fur, and orphaned lentils.

As I'm putting old files and photo albums away, I come across the very first snapshot of me, when I came home from the hospital.

I was born in Addis Ababa, the capital of Ethiopia. My family moved there from India several years before, as my dad's job had demanded.

Dad was a statistician. He worked for the United Nations Population Division and wrote two books on demographics which are, to this day, still Greek to me. Mom worked part-time with the United Nations Women's Guild.

We lived in an apartment block across the road from Haile Selassie, emperor of Ethiopia and Rastafarian messiah.

My sister Subrata, who is ten years older than I am, went to an English school in Addis. We were brought up by two Ethiopian nannies — Heli and Segi.

BEEP

I remember only fragments from our time in Ethiopia: riding go-karts with my sister, the taste of injera, Dusty Springfield and Nana Mouskouri on the stereo, the sweet smell of Segi.

I attended an English kindergarten. Subrata was sent off to boarding school in England when she was 12.

My folks told me I spoke Amharic as a toddler though I only remember a couple of words now: leba, which means "thief" and tinish-tinish, which means "little."

Subrata came back to Addis Ababa during her school holidays. We'd play cardboard records out out of the backs of cereal boxes, build LEGO houses, and read comics.

When I was six, revolution broke out in Ethiopia, which forced the U.N. to resettle us in New York. I don't remember that more but it must have been pretty momentous for my parents.

For the first month or so, we lived in the Roger Smith Hotel on East 47th Street, subsisting on Asian fried chicken takeaway dinners.

Good evening, young miss. How are you finding our fair city?

Eventually we found an apartment in Waterside, a strange complex of four towers clad in red brick, atop an elevated plaza, overlooking the East River.

Do you like the view, beti?

My parents enrolled me at the United Nations International School which was, conveniently enough, about 50 feet from Waterside, which meant, in later years, that I could stumble out of bed 15 minutes before classes started and still be on time.

JUNIOR 1
MS. OLIVEIROS
1975

I was put into a bilingual program for some reason. Half our classes were in French, half in English.

Euh...

mon chat est noir et blanc et il, euh... aime faire des bandes dessinées...

Ah, mais c'est impossible, Anjali! M'enfin, les chats ne savent pas dessiner!

My classmates were from all over the world: Germany, Ghana, Guyana, Guatemala. My best friend in first grade was Yuko, who told me she housed a secret rocket in her basement that her dad would commandeer to the moon on weekends.

... and you can be Colonel Steve.

Why do you always get to be Wonder Woman?

I loved the taste of her mom's Nori rolls.

In second grade, I made friends with a small gang of girls: Gregoria, Kayan, and Francesca.

Somewhat organically, we began drawing comics on 11" x 14" newsprint. We invented a crew of bizarre characters: a sneezy nose with arms and legs, a woman with a bottom for a head.

-ACHOO-

Oh, I say!

OH-OH!

17

We'd often have sleepovers at each other's houses. One time at Francesca's palatial digs on the upper east side, we stole into her parents' bedroom where from a chest of drawers, she dug out from a tiny velvet-lined box, one of her mom's glass eyes.

In fifth grade, we were hanging out on Francesca's bunkbed when she revealed to me the mysteries of The Joy of Sex. I remember... lovingly rendered drawings of very hairy men.

At birthday parties, we'd play "Pass the parcel" and dance to the hits of the day: Shaun Cassidy, Sister Sledge, The Sugar Hill Gang.

Sixth grade meant moving up to the fourth floor of the school. We were all very impressed with the chemistry labs and such,

Once a year, our class would be taken off to New Jersey for "camping" excursions. There was bug juice, trust-building games, apple cobbler, sitting with some of the cool boys during lunch.

I haven't shat in days.

French class got more intense. Our new teacher, Madame Cuvelier, had flaming red hair and an assertive manner. We called her "The Dragon Lady"— she petrified us mightily but I wanted to be like her: bold, confident, sexy.

Et alors, cette pièce de Molière... qu'en penses-tu, Anjali?

Buuuhhh... m'enfin... c'est à dire...

I had taken up the clarinet, under the impression that playing jazz was "cool"—Little did I know that we'd end up playing things like "Ebony and Ivory" and the theme from Rocky in woodwind ensemble instead.

Come on, flutes! Allegro! Get it together!

I continued to make comics under the tutelage of Dorothy, who was a year older than I was and took me under her wing. She used rapidographs for inking (I was still stuck at the pencilling stage) and Zip-a-tone (look it up) for shading.

Whoa! This is, like, so professional!

Just stick with me, kid.

19

In chemistry class, while the other kids were busy with experiments, I'd watch Madame Cuvelier teach French in the classroom across the way.

Hey, are you gonna help with this titration or just gawp at her all day?

I was a pretty shy, dweeby, introverted kid. I exhibited none of the bad behavior that seemed to be mandatory to a high school experience. My pals and I would hang out after school, drinking cokes and snacking on gummy bears and Lik-M-Aid.

The other kids would smoke, drink, pair off, make out. Our nerdiness exempted us from those particular practices.

In the evenings, we'd chat on the phone for hours about homework, computer games, the best strategies for running the dreaded mile in gym class. My friend Harisita's suggestion: just run as fast as you can the whole way, which I did —

Aww GROSS!

Well, clearly that did NOT work out as planned.

only to throw up at the end of it.

In French class, Madame Cuvelier had started to single me out: she lavished praise on me continuously. I would visit her in the modern languages department after school. I'd sit there on the floor, just below the fog of cigarette smoke and gift her with records.

Ah, The Jam! Merci, Anjali — t'es vraiment gentille.

I made a new crew of friends and together we started to get into scary music: Joy Division, Bauhaus, Siouxsie & the Banshees. I began wearing Dr. Martens boots and oversized fuzzy pullovers.

We would go to CBGB's to see ska and hardcore bands. I was starting to feel less dweeby, a little more dangerous.

After classes we'd head off to St. Mark's Place to buy records, T-shirts, and badges, culminating in a pilgrimage to Bleecker Bob's record store in the West Village, with its notoriously surly owner often hovering about.

Whaddaya lookin' fer? Punk? New wave? Gothic? Huh?

I, I, I — I'm just browsing...

Dad seemed to enjoy his work at the U.N. He was always travelling, off to a new destination every few months: Tashkent, Ankara, Geneva, Belgrade. Mom had started doing a Master's at Teacher's College at Columbia and occasionally subbing at my school.

Being proper Bengalis, my folks were obsessed with fish— and the best fish markets were in Chinatown, where Dad would take me on weekends. The Chinese fishmongers got to know him and even picked up a few Bengali phrases from him.

Hello sir... apni kemon achhen?

Bhalo achhi, thank you.

Twice a year we'd go out to New Jersey or Long Island for Durga Puja and Kali Puja, annual festivals honoring fierce Hindu goddesses.

Every couple of months we'd visit my aunt out on Long Island. These were sleepy affairs, the highlight of which was preparing dinner: rice, dal, fried okra, neem leaves, vegetable curry, and, of course, the revered and much-discussed fish entrée.

Can't they see that these excursions into suburbia are KILLING ME?!

My attitude in those days was spectacularly obnoxious.

In 11th grade, Madame Cuvelier invited me over to her apartment on the pretext of returning her dissertation, which she'd lent me over the summer. She answered the door in a nightgown, shooed her kids away, and made us a pot of tea. We chatted for a good while *en Français* about jazz, socialism, my plans for college.

Ah, te voilà, Anjali! Entre, je t'en prie.

I left trembling.

At the advanced age of 18, I kissed a boy for the first time: Timo, a tall German kid who used to date Bergatha, the metal chick in our grade.

What he saw in the likes of me was unclear.

He tasted of cigarettes, which seemed very sexy to me at the time. One time in art class, Frances — who I'd known since second grade— told me:

Timo says you're an *excellent* kisser.

For my final project in art, I drew a short comic (something about dis-affected youth in a record store) and did two paintings that riffed on that comic. I thought I was getting pretty good at art and that I could go on to study fine arts in college.

It's looking so nice, Anju!

Aw! Thanks, Ma.

But my folks urged me to follow my bourgeois Bengali calling and become a doctor instead. I applied to and got into Cornell to study biology. I wasn't at all enthusiastic about this, but I thought I didn't really have a choice.

You can do art in your spare time, Anju.

Graduation day was a bit of a whirl-wind. The ceremony took place in the General Assembly Hall at the United Nations. Bergatha showed up in a formal gown and everyone applauded.

There was a party afterward at some hole in the wall in the East Village and everyone was drunk. Timo broke up with me that day.

Whoa

But I kissed two other boys... and Harisita that night.

In August that year, my aunt and my mom drove me up to Ithaca in a rented station wagon. I sat in the back with all my boxes of clothes and records, and read a letter that my friend Neshama (who I'd known since we were seven) had written me:

It's a scary world out there, Princess. But I know you and I know we can do this.

Day 3 in the life of a newly hatched full-time artist. Ampersand has taken to waking me up at 5:00am. for breakfast.

The leavings from Monday have run out, which means: sautéed cilantro & chard stems & potato with naan for brunch.

Work continues apace. So glad not to be working on bathroom details for Goldman Sachs clients anymore. And thank god, the AutoCAD dreams have stopped.

As 5:00 pm. starts to loom, thoughts veer away from drawing & toward dinner & wine. Will have to conjure up something out of the half an eggplant, tomatoes, & shallots remaining in the fridge. Oh wait... isn't there an entire cabbage in there too?

Ampersand & I watch an English detective show while I polish off the bottle of Syrah from last night. For once, the murderer turns out not to be a vengeful lesbian. Will wonders never cease?

Day 6. Dreams have switched from Auto-CAD to high school exam anxiety, in which I have somehow forgotten to attend math class for the whole semester, much less study for the final exam, which, of course, is tomorrow.

> I can't believe you haven't done any homework all year.

> B-but I-I already have a Master's degree!

Lunch is steamed tofu, lentils, barley, and greens. The customary cup of strong tea precedes the drawing session.

Must buy a new kneaded eraser. The old one is saturated.

I'm liking the story I'm working on. Everything's slowed down so there's time to inhabit the dialogue for a change. Never had the luxury of time enough to create a longer narrative. But will it end up being too chatty? Not enough "action"? Ugh... mustn't second-guess.

Found some frozen tortellini in the freezer, which when combined with a jar of supermarket tomato sauce (augmented with toasted shallots & red chili flakes) and a side of broc rabe, makes for a perfectly acceptable meal.

Out of wine— must resort to the Brooklyn Lager left over in the crisper.

Ugh. Woke up way too late and felt like a slob and a complete loser. Even Ampersand failed to rouse me. What the hell? Maybe it was all that beer. Must replenish wine supply.

Just toast with Marmite, tomatoes & pickle for lunch. Also several cups of tea to reinvigorate. But... did not get out of PJs until noon! Pathetic. Must implement a strict get-dressed code ASAP.

Still averaging a page a day, pencilled. At this rate, it'll take 74 more days to finish pencilling. And then — oh lordy — how much longer to ink & put down gray washes?

Oh geez — do I have enough money to last me that long? What the fuck have I gotten myself into?

Fuck it. I deserve to order in. I'ma get an artichoke & olive pizza.

Oh shit. I is drunk.

27

OK, I think I need to officially get out of the house or else I am officially going to lose it. Plus I need stuff anyway: contact lens solution, toothpaste, cat food, watercolor paper.

I treat myself to a tofu *banh mi* (I know, so 2011) and a lychee soda for lunch. At some point, will have to check my checking account. But maybe not today.

More drawing in the early afternoon, and then couch time with the *Times*. Boy, that A. O. Scott is a real curmudgeon.

Mmmm.... "Cumberbatch."

I go out for a drink with Mala, at the Otter & Trumpet. Mala is a sympathetic listener, but in a consistently OTT manner.

Well, it's a little weird to be home all the time—

No, no... I'm fine!

Oh, no sweetie! Are you feeling lonely? What can I do?

Two weeks into the grand experiment. Cooler temperatures mean an extra blanket at night and extra canoodling with Ampersand.

And yet—gawd—I shouldn't be lying in bed until 9:30—that's just...sad. Maybe I need a new routine. Or maybe I should stop over-analyzing myself.

Thirteen pages pencilled. I take a break to post a page on Facebook and get 20 likes in an hour. Even Colin O'Connor, who is usually full of bile and cutting wit, is all like "Anjali, this looks great!," exclamation mark and all.

Well, if it isn't the queen of gloom herself now!

Ah, shut it, Colin.

Instead of resorting to a drink in the evening, I try a series of Sun Salutations instead. Which is oddly fulfilling. Maybe... maybe I could incorporate this into my morning routine instead of sleeping all the time?

The best days start early, when I have to draw the curtains against the direct morning sun. I listen to the BBC world service and sip a mug of strong tea.

Tensions continue to escalate in the midlands after the announcement of this year's regional shed of the year competition winners...

I take a look at the 120 pages of comics I've done already. Stuff I worked on during the — gasp! — 10 years I was at Chad's office, in my spare time. Some stories that have been published in alt-comix anthologies, some which have remained hidden all these years.

At 4:00 pm. yoga class, I'm approached by a blond girl I've noticed before at the studio.

Hey! You're Anjali, right? I just wanted to introduce myself — I'm Tina.

Oh! Hi — it's... so nice to meet you, Tina.

As I'm preparing a salad for dinner, I am horrified to discover a snail in among the spinach leaves. I'm reminded of the time there was a slug happily squirming away in the lettuce at the salad bar in the dining hall my first semester of college — and how misplaced and lonely I was that year.

Hellloooooo

So, being an unformed girl of 18, I went along with my parents' plans for my career and went to an Ivy League school to study biology on a pre-med track.

What's wrong?

I didn't make it past 2nd semester bio lab. It was the fetal pigs that did me in.

I switched to an interior design program. My mother accepted this begrudgingly when I told her I could do my graduate studies in architecture. She was not exactly forthcoming with the truth of my situation with everyone, though.

Aaré, I thought she was doing pre-med, na?

She's studying interior architecture.

It's interior _design_, Ma.

ARCHITECTURE!

Senior year in college, I hit the jackpot.

Baba, guess what? I got into the graduate architecture program at Harvard!

I always knew you could do it, beti.

Finally Ma & Baba would have something to brag about.

Oh, Vikram? Such a good boy. Now he is doing engineering at Columbia.

Achha? Well done. Our Anjali was only just now accepted to

HARVARD

31

And that was ok. Because I had a pretty great time in grad school — I learned to think expansively and sideways and diagonally. I tried mightily to absorb Derrida, Eisenman, Deleuze, Koolhaas — and to somehow incorporate such seemingly radical thinking into my projects.

Ciggie break?

Fuck that shit— let's go to Casa-blanca and get smashed!

Uh... the waste water from the hydro-nautic research facility is directed through a series of pneumatic sluices in an attempt to challenge the master narrative and patriarchical hegemony of modernism and, uh...

But more often than not, my presentations ended up sounding more like Monty Python sketches,

I moved back to New York after graduation and landed a job at I.M. Pei's office, which gave my folks even more bragging rights.

Anjali helped to design the Louvre museum in Paris!

I sure did not do that thing.

3 years later I was lured away by Chad (who was then a senior associate at Pei's) to join his private practice. At the time, it seemed like a good idea— I was making more money, the work was smaller scale, the atmosphere was laid-back, and I made good friends.

Beer o'clock?

Hell yeah.

For the most part, the ensuing years were low-key and pleasant. But with every year, my interest in architecture waned, dramatically. You can only get so excited about compiling binders of plumbing fixtures and drawing details of pantry cabinets.

ooh. hoo hoo hoo ♪♫

*sigh... I bet Kate Bush never suffered the indignity of having to endure such soul-crushing tedium.

Chad deteriorated psychologically in short order, particularly after dealing with one rather nasty Wall Street client and her Central Park South luxury loft.

The stone in the foyer is completely unacceptable! How can you expect me to live like this?!

Try to calm down, Susan.

He descended into a Lunesta and Chassagne-Montrachet (2003) vortex and rarely showed up to the office or to meetings.

Chad? It's Anjali..., it's 11:00!

Who... who is this?

It's Anjali! You were supposed to be at the job site at 10:00!

Ah... remind me why?

The projects slowed down and dried up. Chad barely made an effort to pursue new work.

Too bad... we can't afford paper towels anymore.

And then of course there was the whole health insurance debacle.

Why, my physician doesn't even accept health insurance!

HA HA HA

Chad was running the office into the ground but didn't have the courage to have an honest conversation with his employees about our situation.

So we're losing the lease on the office space?

Yes, but don't worry—we'll just move all the computers to my apartment.

And that was when I felt everything converge, as if lord Krishna himself was telling me:

Anjali, you have to get out of this place. Do what you were meant to do. Go on—write your graphic novel—that is what you call them these days, isn't it?

...hello...?

And like a holy fool, I heeded the voice of Krishna.

What part of "I fucking quit" do you not get?!

Well it's what I'm good at and it's what I want to do with my—

Wait, you can actually afford to take a whole year off?

Um, yeah... like I said, my dad and my aunt left me some money so I thought—

Oh, my god — so you have the luxury of not working for an entire year and you're bitching about going a "little stir-crazy"?

Um, it's not like I'm lazing around — I'm writing and drawing every day and I will have a book at the end of it all—

Uh, yeah... meanwhile the rest of us have to go to an office and make money to pay the rent because we don't have inheritances. Hello?!

Now wait a minute — And you actually make lunch out of chard stems and broccoli stalks because you feel guilty for being rich?

OMG, #firstworldproblems.

Have you ever had to wipe your mother's ass because her brain is so riddled with Alzheimer's that she can't even go to the bathroom by herself?

Or, pray tell, have you ever sat by helplessly witnessing your father sink into depression, lassitude, and obesity only to be thousands of miles away, conveniently absent when he dies, in his bed, alone, on fucking Christmas day?

Have you had the distinct pleasure of watching your aunt, the only family you have left in this country, waste away because her anal cancer has exploded and travelled north where it is eating away at her stomach and intestines which means when she's not knocked out by pain meds, she's spewing up red bloody vomit every couple of hours?

Have you ever heard a fucking death rattle?!

No? Well, I have, motherfucker. So maybe, just maybe, it's ok for me to reassess my life choices and actually do what I'm good at, given the financial possibility of doing so,

Considering I have no family left and that I'm pretty much ALONE in this world, guess what? I'm not gonna feel guilty about coming into some money. I'm gonna kick career opportunities in the ass, write a fat-ass graphic novel and be free to complain that YEAH, I sometimes do get lonely! ALL without needing your fucking approval!

Oh, my god, what a bitch.

And why don't you stick your #hashtag up your beardy hipster ass!

Ok, so I can actually do this. 9:30 yoga class is an absolute wonder and I feel better about myself for a change, despite hamstrings like taut rubber bands, crazy shaking quads, and a supremely wobbly tree pose.

Après-yoga brunch is a delight even though it is yet again just leavings. Will make a point of going to yoga regularly from now on. At the very least, even if I don't get very far on the road to Samadhi, I will have travelled some ways away from Loserville.

The characters in the story I'm working on are really beginning to grow on me, despite and because of their many foibles and short-comings. Still too much dialogue maybe but whatever... people need to read more.

Can I make it two nights sans vin rouge?

Three weeks in now. Been trying to wake up at 8:00, which is late for most working people — I realize this — but have been failing often. There are days I would like to will myself into a dream and stay there for most of the morning.

Oh, sweet sweet sleep.

I get an email around lunchtime from an old work colleague (who has heard that I've left Chad's office) and is starting up his own architectural practice and would I like to have lunch with him soon?

My first reaction is to run screaming — I didn't even like this guy that much and the last thing I need is yet another toxic work environment — but should I really say no to making a little extra money? Plus I'd get out of the house which would be good for my oh-so-fragile mental state.

I email him in the afternoon and say sure, let's meet next week. Hell, I don't have to commit to anything, do I?

No, I certainly do not, Monsieur Ampersand!

Dinner is leftover veg pullao, saag with tofu, and a particularly jaunty Spanish red that tastes like dill.

Four weeks in. Not doing so badly with maintaining the semblance of a schedule. Mornings when I can guilt myself into it, I do 20 sun salutations. Even though my arms hit the bookshelves when I dive down into Uttanasana.

So I'm meeting that old work colleague tomorrow. I decide to look through the architectural port-folio that I cobbled together in the dying days of Chad's office. Oh look— details for the 12-seater Jacuzzi in the Florida pleasure palace. Goldman Sachs can have pulsating jets on his upper, middle, & lower back.

I should have located a jet to direct a high-velocity bubble stream straight up Goldman's bottom.

Well, I'm not gonna sweat it. Anyway, the more important thing is to get the book done. With some extra-concerted effort, I'm somehow up to 40 pencilled pages.

I feel a reward coming on.

After dinner, Ampersand gets salmon treats and I get a Rioja treat, while we sit on the floor, discussing music.

I don't know, Ampersand... it's not as innovative as *Loveless*... but how could anything be?

My meeting with Eric Butcher (who was at Chad's office for many years but flew the coop to do his own thing) goes well— he's much more affable than I remember and wants to know if I'd like to do some work for him.

I say sure, why not? Eric says he'll call me in a month when he's ready to start producing drawings.

I get to feel like I'm "getting things done" because I'm riding the Ⓕ train in and out of Manhattan.

Flush with the possibility of making money and not feeling so much like a layabout, I apply myself doubly to focusing on drawing, thinking it is an even nobler endeavor when done in parallel with the business of financial maintenance.

As the sun starts to set, I go for a walk in Prospect Park. It's warm enough for a Chocolate lab and a chihuahua to be cavorting at Dog Beach, but the air is still nippy & bracing, like I imagine it is in Edinburgh or Stockholm.

There is something really wrong with me. Or: everyone else is de-volving into a new species of self-centered, braying, enduringly nasty bipeds. I'd like to blame technology but that's too easy... science has just enabled people to fully become the assholes they always were.

Yes — you already knew this — that commuting inflames one's mis-anthropy. But what to do? I'll turn myself into a gibbering idiot if I work from home any longer, stewing myself into grand sulks in between illustration gigs.

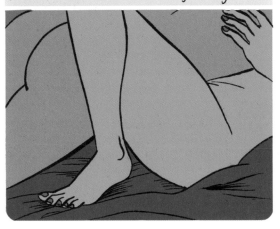

"Woe is thee" you're thinking, cry me a river. Well, I'm sure you get tired of counting your blessings too matey — or else you are a holy fool of the highest order, and I have several lifetimes to go before I can catch up with your piety.

Oh, what the hell — maybe they'll invent a dampening field in the future. Too late to quell my bad attitude but perhaps there will be hope for future generations of mis-shapes. In the meantime, if you know of any invocations against boorishness and stupidity, please let me know.

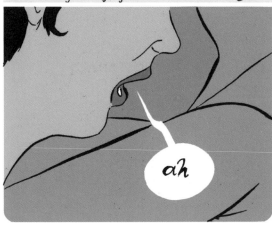

At morning yoga, Tina tells me she's hung over. I tell her I'm a little wobbly too. She suggests we should meet up for a drink since ... we both like to drink. I say yes a little too easily.

As I spend the afternoon drawing, I wonder if there is even a market for the kind of comics I'm doing: no superheroes, robots, zombies, vampires. Should I throw in a pirate or ninja character to align myself with the zeitgeist?

I think about my parents and what they would have made of my career diversion. No doubt they would have disapproved. Even so, I'm hopeful. If this whole book thing works out, I think they'd have been proud of me.

For dinner, I make a simple Indian meal: rice, fried eggplant, and dal, the way Mom and Dad used to make it, with both moong and masoor lentils, and frozen peas toward the end. It's never quite as good as the way they did it, though.

Do you want some dal, sweetie? It's part of your Indian heritage!

When I moved back to New York after grad school, I'd go see my folks on weekends for Bengali home cooking, gossip about relatives back in India, and lots of naps. Dad was enjoying his retirement and Mom was teaching ESL.

I felt myself gliding easily into my late twenties — I was being fed and babied on weekends, work was a breeze... what did I care about?

Have some more dal, beti.

I'm totally full, Ma.

Eat, beti, eat!

I'm going out with Mala, you guys.

Wear your gloves, Anju!

Don't have too much fun.

After a Saturday night out in the East Village, I'd sleep in late, huddled up in my childhood bed. Dad would make rice & lentil stew for brunch and Ma would make spinach with mustard oil.

But as Dad always used to say, "when men make plans, God laughs." Mom became ever more forgetful, unsure, & agitated. Dad couldn't even bring himself to say it out loud. He called it the 'A' word.

You see, when the rice and lentils are cooked *together*, the nutritional properties of both are boosted — it's just chemistry!

Uh-huh.

Dad had even begun to compile our family recipes into a cookbook.

Grrrrrrrrr

They're right here, Ma.

44

The diagnosis became official. Mom quit teaching. At the time, she could still cook, take care of herself, do the laundry — although sometimes it would take her 4 hours to do a small load. My god, I even left her alone to go to parties when Dad was travelling.

Are you sure you'll be ok alone?

Of course, beti... you go have fun.

The wonder of it — she could communicate with me back then.

But Ma's memory gradually started flickering out. She forgot the names of objects and what they were for. She sometimes put her clothes on in the wrong order. Sometimes she just seemed ... lost.

What are you looking for, Ma?

The ... the thing.

What thing?

The ... thing! The round thing!

It very quickly got to this point:

What do you call this, Ma?

The East River.

Yeah! And who am I?

... related.

Well, clearly we're related! But what's my name?

...

One night when Mom and Dad were invited to a dinner party in our building, we all did a victory dance when it turned out Mom was still able to tie her sari properly. They went off triumphantly to Mrs. Sen's house, with some baked mushroom rolls that I'd devised.

Yay! I knew you could do it, Ma!

Come on — the samosas will get cold!

I celebrated by ordering take-out and watching shitty TV. But soon enough, Mom was escorted home as she'd started to feel self-conscious and scared by not being able to interact with her friends like she used to.

Thanks for bringing her up, Rupa.

I spent the rest of the evening with her on the sofa, watching The X-Files.

Mulder, are you saying you actually *believe* this was the work of giant vampiric caterpillars?

Miraculously, Mom started to improve after that episode. No, of course she didn't. I started to spend nights with her in bed in case she had to get up to pee, which she had to do quite often. Sometimes, if I was asleep, she wouldn't even make it to the toilet.

Again?!

I didn't sleep very well for a month.

Eventually, my older sister (who had flown in from London), my dad, and I settled on a long-term plan: move Mom and Dad back to India, where they could afford 24-hour private care.

I can't believe this is happening.

Oh, grow up.

Can we *focus*, please?

The process of uprooting was, of course, painful. We'd lived in that apartment since 1974, and the decor in my room hadn't changed since high school. Suddenly, every object in the place was suffused with memory and sadness.

In October of 2000, we all braved the 25 hour journey to Kolkata where my folks grew up and owned a flat. Mom was understandably agitated & frightened, despite the valium. Dad insisted that I trade places with him in business class.

Please, beti → you go. I can't take it anymore. Anyway, she likes you best.

just so I could be in charge of accompanying Mom to the bathroom, which ended up being a very awkward tango for both of us every 20 minutes.

Goddamnit! I thought business-class johns were supposed to be bigger!

We installed Mom & Dad in the flat they'd owned for decades and hired day & night nurses for Mom. The day nurse, along with the cook we'd hired, also cleaned the flat. It was an oddly comforting atmosphere because things finally seemed under control.

Eat one more piece of fish, young Miss!

I'm not young but I am going to explode.

Well, everything except the rampant spread of tangled plaque in Ma's brain.

Ma would often get very agitated with her nurses. I guess she knew she was ill, but having nurses around, treating her like an invalid, just brought the point home.

God! Cut it out! She's only here to help you!

The nurses were great and took good care of Ma. Well, of course there was also the night nurse Mary who would try to convert Ma while she slept.

"Come to me, all you who are weary and burdened, and I will give you rest..."

Oh Ma Durga... save me from this bible-thumper

Somehow making the journey to India had done further damage to Ma's powers of speech. She hardly said anything anymore. But, wonder of wonders, she was still able, if urged on, to sing the Indian national anthem.

Jana gana mana Adhinaayak jeya hai, Bhaarat bhaagya vidhataa...

VANDE MATARAM!

Our relatives had heard about Ma's condition well in advance and would come by the flat to pay their respects. Even Ma's sisters would come, if rather hesitatingly— they were, obviously, not eager to peer into their own potential futures.

Oh Kona! Won't you say something? It's me, your Manika!

48

We settled into a routine—after the obligatory afternoon nap, we'd take Ma out for a walk in the park across the road from our flat.

Doctors would come regularly to pay—gasp!—house calls for Ma.

Anjali, show Doctor Babu down to his car.

Really?

Oh, you don't need to—

Don't argue!

After dinner, we'd settle down to watch trashy Bengali serials on TV. Sometimes my aunt would come over to watch the Hindi version of *Who Wants to Be a Millionaire?*

Main kaun hoon?

Aishwarya Rai! No, no... Bill Clinton!

Owing to jet lag, I would read Baba's old Ruth Rendell novels well into the small hours.

I hadn't been back to India since I was 18, when we'd come over on summer vacation. Back then, I'd count the days until we could go back to New York. But now I was enjoying all our old rituals.

And after such a hiatus, it was comforting to see my cousins, aunts, & uncles again when they'd come to our flat, unannounced.

Of course, coming back to India after so many years also had its downside.

I wasn't counting days anymore. Time sped up strangely that year, unlike a lot of Kolkata, which ambled along languorously. (Manic taxis excluded.)

A month breezed by. After we'd settled Ma & Baba into a comfortable daily routine, it was time to go back.

I'll be back again very soon, Ma.

I was happy to be back in my world of creature comforts, cold weather, & Rioja — I hadn't touched a drop of drink for a month — but leaving Ma & Baba alone for another year made me feel sick. They were both old and so vulnerable.

But sure enough, I'd be back in the Motherland again the next year.

So how is Ma doing, Baba?

Worse than last year, of course, beti. She doesn't say very much and cannot walk as easily. But the strangest thing, Anju, is that once in a while she'll have this startling flash of lucidity.

I want to kiss you.

Of course Ma's condition would only get worse with time. But some things did not change.

How many pieces of fish did you get, Anju?

God! What does it matter?!

Eat one more piece, Miss— you're wasting away!

Saying goodbye to Ma became more difficult every year.

I'll see you really soon, OK, Ma?

In 2001, I don't think she even understood that I was leaving.

When I came back to visit in 2002, Ma couldn't speak at all and was confined to a wheelchair.

Look, darling → Anjali's come to be with you for three weeks! Aren't you going to say hello?

She'd forgotten my name a while ago, but now she couldn't even acknowledge my presence.

Oh, Ma.

And she'd become ever more skeletal.

Somehow we all dealt with our situation — if not bravely, then with a certain resignation.

What choice did we have?

Toward the end, Ma couldn't even get out of bed and had to be fed intravenously and even so was wasting away.

She died in 2003.

At first, things were surprisingly OK between all of us—maybe because we'd been preparing for Ma's death for so long.

My compliments to the chef.

Thank you, Saab.

AND TWO MORE BEERS!

We focused all our attention on Baba.

But with Ma gone, Baba didn't know what to do with himself. He would stay in bed most of the day and only looked forward to dinner and TV Time.

Anju, go ask cook what kind of fish she got from the market for dinner.

Again with the fish?!

The doctors (whom Baba held in the highest esteem) would tell him he needed to get out and exercise and eat healthier foods, but to little avail.

Rana babu, you have to take at least a small walk every day!

Hmm... Anyway, as I was saying, Anjali here graduated from HARVARD...

Baba was even assigned a nutritionist, who, ironically, only made matters worse.

Rana babu, I've brought you some butter chicken!

Ah! Thank you very much, Dr. Mitra!

You have got to be fucking kidding me.

It was an inevitable and quick descent. Without Ma to focus his attention, Baba had just stopped trying, in all aspects of his life.

Come on, Baba, let's just walk to the paanwallah's stall!

Leave me alone.

I felt even worse going home that year, leaving Baba alone.

Please take care of yourself, Baba.

I'll try, beti.

A couple of weeks after coming home to Brooklyn, I called Baba on a snowy December evening. I couldn't understand half of what he was saying to me. About the only thing he could enunciate clearly was:

Please, won't you get married soon, beti?

Oh, god.

And guess what? Baba died the next day. Oh yeah, it was Christmas morning.

I flew out to India the next week, only a month after I'd left it.

After Baba's remembrance service, I accompanied a gaggle of uncles to deposit his ashes by the banks of the Ganges.

No, no...! Take the flyover!

It's down this alley!

I'm telling you, we turn left! You think I don't know where Ma Ganga resides?!

And after that excursion, my sister and I had to feed all the relatives who'd shown up to the service.

Have some more aloo, Anjali →

Tomorrow, we'll get some fish at the market.

God! Do you people think of anything besides FISH?!

We spent the rest of our stay there dealing with the aftermath → Baba's estate, the Kolkata flat, all our parents' belongings, and all the Indian bureaucracy that accompanied these endeavors.

Please to obtain one registered affidavit per item and to sign all 86 documents in triplicate →

Which meant trawling through bills, receipts, letters, wills, contracts—
and albums and albums full of photos.

Oh, my god! It's Ma & Baba when they lived in Ceylon! They were probably just still in their 20s, for god's sake! Baba looks like he lives in Williamsburg!

Jesus! We don't have time for sentimentality just now! Don't think about it—just chuck it in the rubbish—be ruthless!

Having to throw away most of Ma & Baba's stuff—I saved what I could despite my sister's protests—meant there really was nothing left of them. The evidence of two lives lived, 80 years' worth, was now just so much fodder for the scrap heap.

UN in Spotlight

When I wasn't sifting through decades' worth of papers, books, and photos, I'd watch Kolkata buzz along, from our balcony — the honking of horns, the street hawkers' shouts, the circling crows.

At night, I'd read the Ruth Rendell novel I'd had autographed by Baroness Ruth herself to give to Baba — he never managed to finish it,

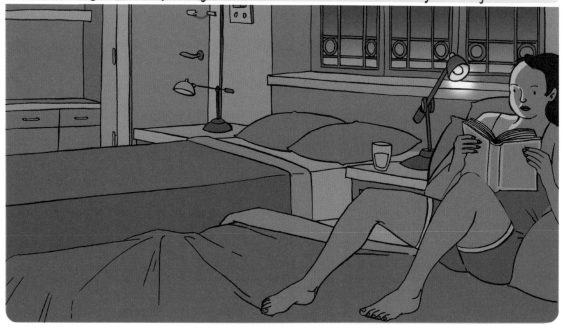

I had to leave a week later. My sister stayed to carry on the long and thankless work of sorting out all of Baba's stuff and dealing with setting the flat.

Have a safe flight, little sis. It's all going to be ok.

Is it?

I'm so sorry, Darwan ji — could you please unlock the gate? I have a plane to catch and my car is waiting outside...

Inevitably, my flight home was at 7:00 a.m., which meant a 3:00 a.m. drive to the airport, unencumbered by traffic, wild dogs, or sacred cows.

I'd always found this drive extraordinarily exciting as a kid because it was the first leg of a flight away from heat, humidity, and filth.

This year, I just felt a strange soothing numbness.

I also loved setting off on voyages. Baba would type up packing lists on 5" x 7" index cards, and we'd drive to JFK in a Cadillac car service,

I'd poke around the duty-free shops and absorb the aroma of asafoetida-laced packed lunches in the Air India lounge,

We'd travel to India every two years, stopping at fancy places on the way there and back — Madrid, Moscow, Paris, Prague,

We'd also stop in London to see my sister. We stayed in a poky but cozy 8-unit hotel in Earl's Court and get oily takeaway dinners from the Pakistani corner store.

Everything — shopping at the supermarket, travelling on the underground, even watching the evening news — seemed magical when we were abroad.

This one time when I was 8 and we were on our way to India, I sat next to this elegant Pakistani woman on the plane—she was very sweet and chatted with me the entire trip. We had a 3-hour layover in Bahrain for refuelling and she asked Ma & Baba if she could take me for a walk through the airport, just to relieve the tedium,

God knows why they agreed (I could have easily been kidnapped and whisked off to some stylish demimonde) but they did — and this mondaine took me by the hand and led me around the luxury boutiques, pretending to shop for Gucci handbags and Chanel No. 5. She brought me back to the plane after an hour and I thought, my god, I've graduated right out of childhood.

Where to, Miss?

Park Slope, please.

I stopped travelling with Ma & Baba after I entered college. But I spent a lot of time after that trying to re-create that magic. I'd draw maps of fictional cities and floor plans of imaginary hotels. I could pore over the London tube map and wish myself into its magical stations — Angel, Blackfriars, Chalk Farm, Seven Sisters.

Fleeting pleasures, to be sure — but these pursuits tethered me to a faith.

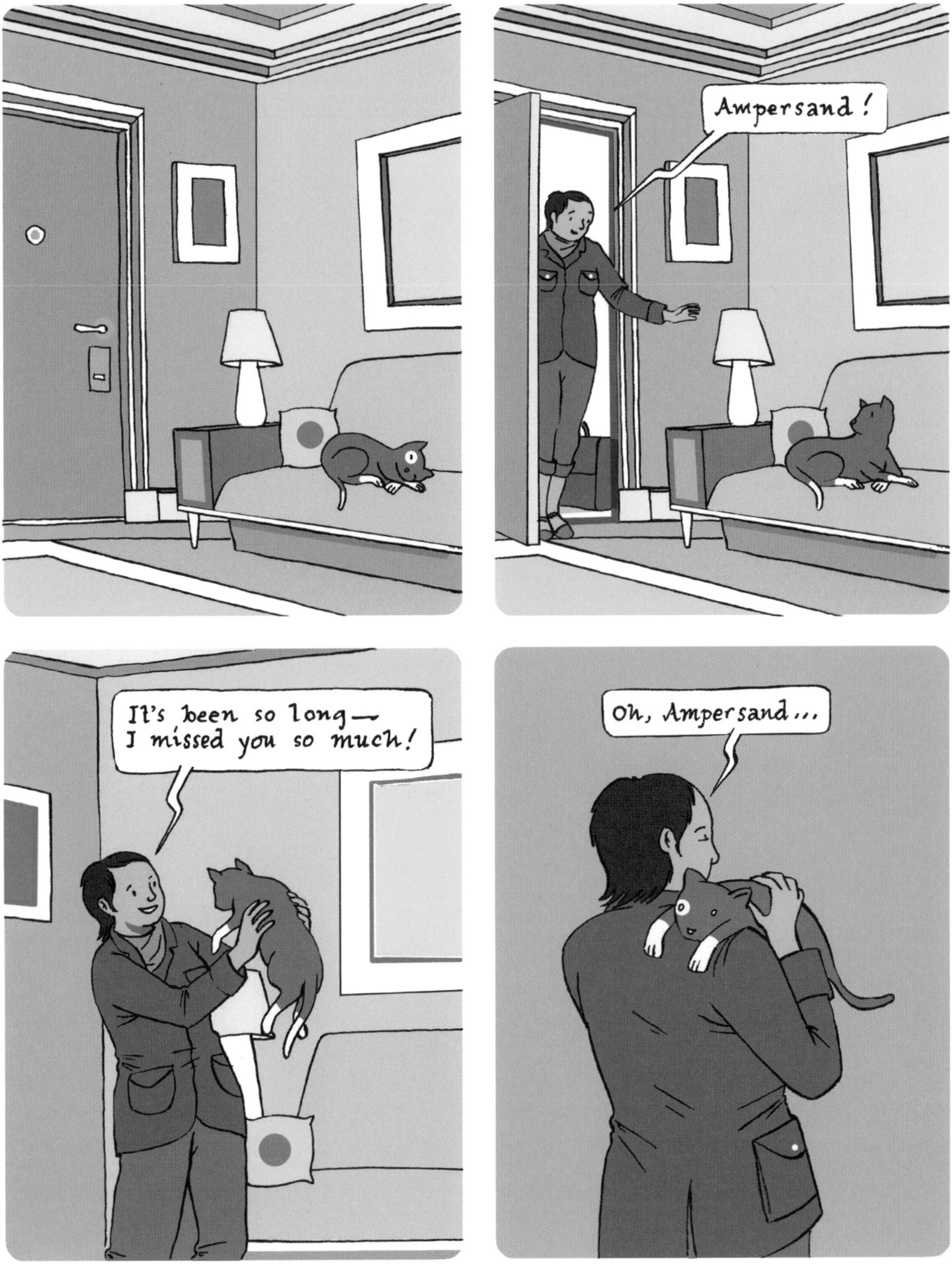
Ampersand!
It's been so long— I missed you so much!
Oh, Ampersand...

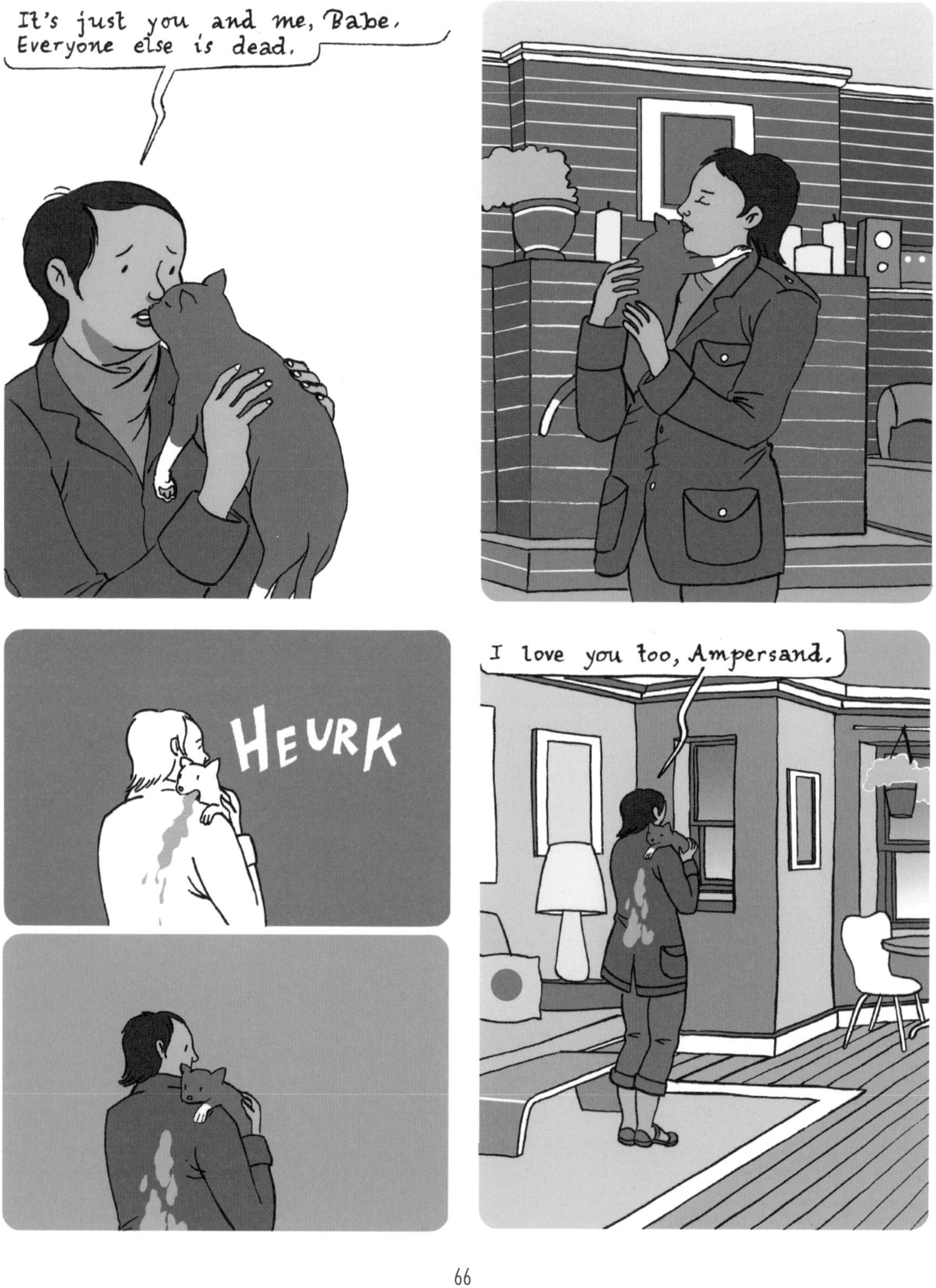
It's just you and me, Babe. Everyone else is dead.
HEURK
I love you too, Ampersand.

So guess what? No, guess. No, it doesn't involve murder. It's this — I am done, DONE, with pencilling this comic, all 80 pages of it.

I can hardly believe it. I barely know what to do with myself.

Arati begrudgingly agrees to come out with me to the Otter & Trumpet to mark the occasion. Though she's not exactly sure what the big deal is.

It took you how long to do what?

You can probably guess how the evening ends.

Oh, Goddess! Wh— what have I done with my life? Who the hell draws comics f-for a "living"?!

Pencils behind me, I'm on two weeks of inking now. It had been so long since I handled a brush that I've been tentative with it but I feel the muscle memory returning.

Inking seems to be, thankfully, going faster than pencilling, since I'm not expending time setting up and fussing over panels.

IT'S JUST... ALL SO SUDDEN!

DIDN'T YOU KNOW ALL ALONG?

Before you know it, it's 6:00 p.m. My vision's a little wobbly when I get up to feed Ampersand. My hand is all cramped up.

SLORP GLORP

It's a lonely business, that it is— but such is the nature of art.

Wouldn't you agree, Mr. Beckett?

Ah, 'tis a fool's game, to be sure, Miss Anjali.

People are so gross. I mean, really— a ten minute walk through midtown Manhattan is enough to make you go running for the nearest convent or turn into an axe murderer. It's all you can do to keep from just curling up into a little cocoon to ward off the outside world.

Seriously, what the fuck— people in cars barrelling down streets like they're in a fucking *Fast & Furious* movie? Screeching harpies screeching into their iPhones about the inane details of their life? The horrid masses tossing their Doritos packages shamelessly onto the sidewalk? Men leering, women flaunting— God, this species is fucked.

Is everyone insane? Or just callous to the fact of having to live among other people? Why would you deliberately want to make the world an uglier place? Do they have ugliness and litter and bad footwear and screeching harpies in Switzerland?

Wouldn't it be great to be one of those alien species on *Star Trek* that are pure energy or light? They don't drive Escalades or start wars or eat other light-energy entities. I would be happy as a dolphin too. Or a cat. Then Ampersand and I could groom each other.

Rupture

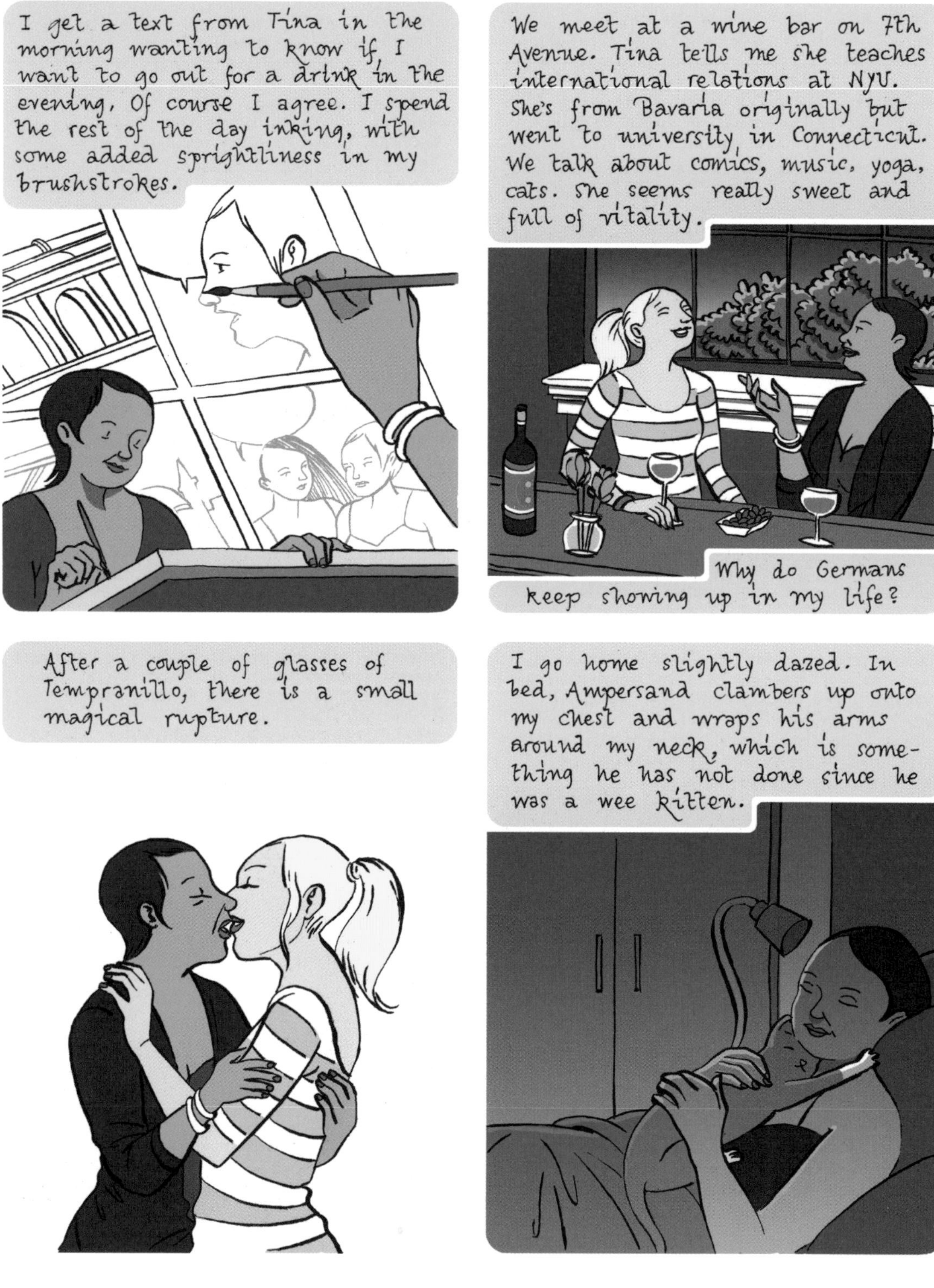
I get a text from Tina in the morning wanting to know if I want to go out for a drink in the evening, Of course I agree. I spend the rest of the day inking, with some added sprightliness in my brushstrokes.
We meet at a wine bar on 7th Avenue. Tina tells me she teaches international relations at NYU. She's from Bavaria originally but went to university in Connecticut. We talk about comics, music, yoga, cats. She seems really sweet and full of vitality.
Why do Germans keep showing up in my life?
After a couple of glasses of Tempranillo, there is a small magical rupture.
I go home slightly dazed. In bed, Ampersand clambers up onto my chest and wraps his arms around my neck, which is something he has not done since he was a wee kitten.

When I first moved to Park Slope after grad school, I rented a one-bedroom apartment on 7th Street. The super there was a cat-loving Cuban-American Republican.

Hi, Sammy. Please don't turn the hose on me.

He took care of the neighborhood strays, one of which lived in the back yard of another building that he maintained.

She has kittens! You want a kitten?

WHAT?

Six weeks later:

OK, kittens are ready! I pick one out for you!

Now wait a minute—!

I had to run over to the mama cat's yard, where Sammy was waiting for me, kitten in hand.

You like this one? He got attitude.

71

I brought the kitten home even though I felt like I had been press-ganged into it.

I'm sorry to take you away from your mama, but it's no life out there for a wee kitty, dodging cars and nasty birds of prey and whatnot.

He immediately ran under the couch. I set out a bowl of water, a cup of kitten kibble, and a pie tin full of litter.

I tried to coax him out, but to little avail.

Oh c'mon out, little one.

Later that night, as I was watching *Star Trek: Voyager*, the young master deigned to emerge from his dusty hideaway.

Well hello there, baby! Have you managed to escape from the Delta Quadrant?

It didn't take too long for him to get used to his new home and to me.

Well now! This is a first!

I still couldn't think of a good name for him though. On the short list: Desmond, Roland, Tarquin, and... Cymbeline, King of Britain.

I called Priya to tell her about the new addition to my household.

Yeah, he's pretty much litterbox-trained already.

Aw, I was hoping to get to see him in little Pampers, and—

WAIT!

What did you just say?

I said I wanted to see him in little Pampers, and—

Hello?

roo roo?

!

And thusly was he christened.

I text Tina to tell her I had a really nice time and would she like to hang out again soon? All the while I'm not sure of where this is going, if anywhere at all.

Trying not to focus too much on her while inking, I distract myself, listening to a radio documentary about the digging of escape tunnels underneath the Berlin Wall in 1962.

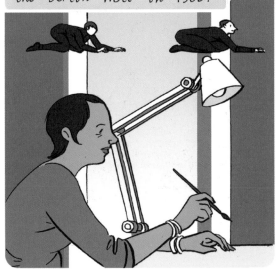

Three more pages of inking done, I make a trip to the Bangladeshi grocery on Church Avenue where I buy tiny eggplants, winter melon, spinach, mustard oil. The shopkeepers know me by now.

Ah! Apni kemon achhen, miss?

Ami khoob bhalo achhi, thank you!

No response from Tina yet. Which maybe doesn't mean all that much. Or maybe it does. I'm tempted to text her again but that would just make me look desperate.

Two weeks later, I'm done inking. I averaged 2 pages of inking a day for a month there, minus blackout days after one too many glasses of Garnacha.

Yes!

(Note to self : stop drinking.)

Priya emails me in the afternoon. Priya, of the long hair and bangs, with her Stevie Nicks shawls and witchy demeanor in college. She says would I want to come up and visit her in the Adirondacks?

Because inks are behind me, and because I think I deserve it, I say yes. I book a ticket for the 12:30 Ethan Allen express train to Albany, where she'll pick me up.

To celebrate, I go to Church Avenue and buy bitter gourds to make Uchche Chachori, just like Mom and Dad used to make. And what goes better with that than a bottle of Chateau "Note to Self" 2019?

Auntie Ingrid will take very good care of you while I'm upstate fighting off black flies, sweetie.

Next stop, Croton-Harmon, 20 minutes

So Dude, what is up with these new shatterproof Olde English bottles?

Bro, you mean that plastic shit? That is, like, so gay.

I know, dude → the whole point is to toss that shit once you're good and fucked up and watch it shatter!

Serious!

I was at the bodega yesterday and I saw that and I was, like, "OE in a plastic bottle?!" Now that is some "WEAK faggot-ass shit, bro!

Exclusively for pussies.

No doubt! I am not down with that gayness, dude.

Bitches and beer, Bro, that's what it's all ab **AAAAHHHHH**

Bro, I literally slept with, like, 17 girls my freshman year!

DAMN bro! Hittin' it like a hammer there, stud!

See, Anj? Isn't this idyllic?

It's been nothing but idyllic this weekend. Well, except for those two assholes on the train.

Oh, forget about them. Your misanthropy has no home out here. It's just you, me, the owls, egrets, moose, possums...

Don't forget the deer ticks.

Oh, you!

Oh, me.

Anj, you should totally quit your part-time job and move up here with me. Think of the expanded hunting opportunities for Ampersand!

He's a city cat at heart — he wouldn't know what to make of wild turkeys. Anyway, what would I do up here? Bag groceries at Price Chopper?

The Price Chopper is in Glens Falls, honey — not the Adirondacks. No, we could — I don't know — start a farm stand!

Hmmm... the vegetables I can deal with. It's the interacting with humans that I would suck at.

77

Oh criminy! A month of mountain living will exorcise that bad attitude right out of you. Look, seriously, forget about architecture for a while, come up here, work on your comics... it'll be amazing!

Well, Priya, my dear, if I didn't need the money from this part-time job and my freelance gigs, I would happily do just that but my trust fund will only take me so far. Anyway, I'm too fond of bars and gigs and MoMA to quit city life.

Oh, suit yourself. Maybe if you marry me, I'll consider moving.

Oho! Setting the bar pretty high there, Anj!

That's how I roll!

Don't you ever get lonely up here?

Not really. I see Jen and Yuko at the arts center every week and I have dinner with Maryam quite often. Anyway, my days of partying and hanging out at bars are behind me.

Are you calling me a drunk?!

Who said anything about you? But sure, you've got your rhythm and I've got mine. I'll take sighting ospreys and going canoeing over slogging it out on the G train any day.

Well, nice work if you can get it.

I do actually have to work to be able to live here, Anj! Anyway, why are you so concerned with being lonely? You don't even like people!

Well, yes... but that doesn't mean I don't require a certain degree of adoration and wooing.

I will woo you every night, with wine and pakoras.

Promises, promises.

Hey, look! We approach the sacred mound of the twin birches, where the wee folk reside and hold revelry in the fullness of moonlight. Magical, no?

Yes, Lord Brahma certainly was in winning form when he dreamed this up.

You realize this means we're nearing our destination, right?

I should hope so— I'm starting to schvitz a little.

And...

...here...

we...

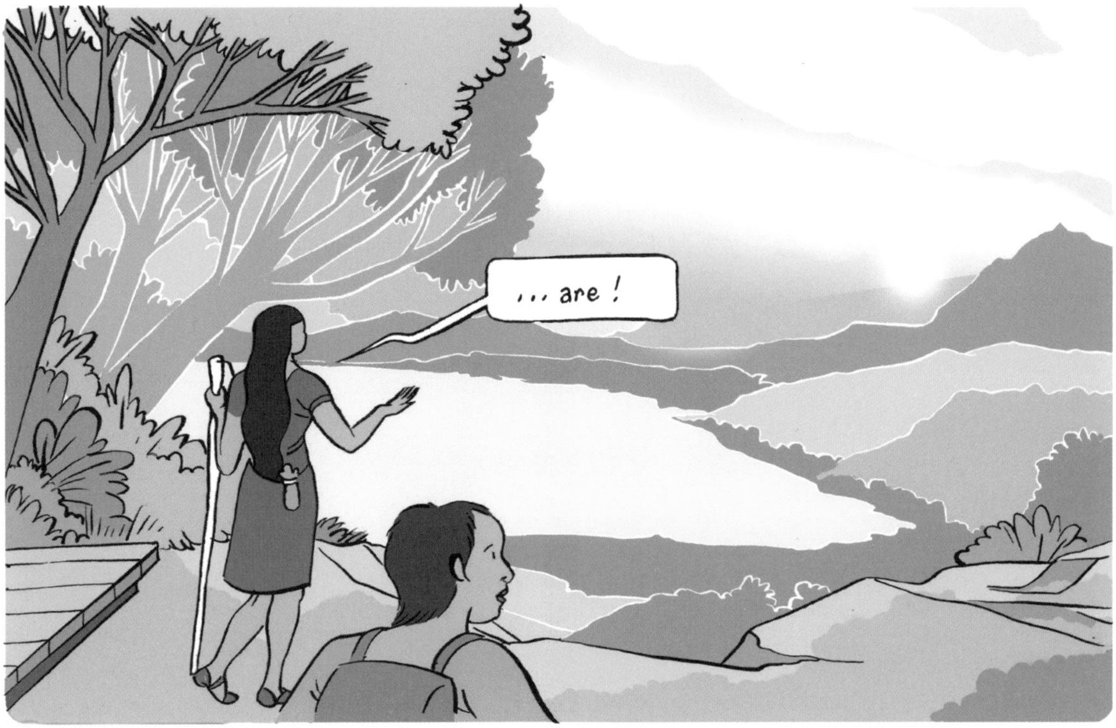
... are !
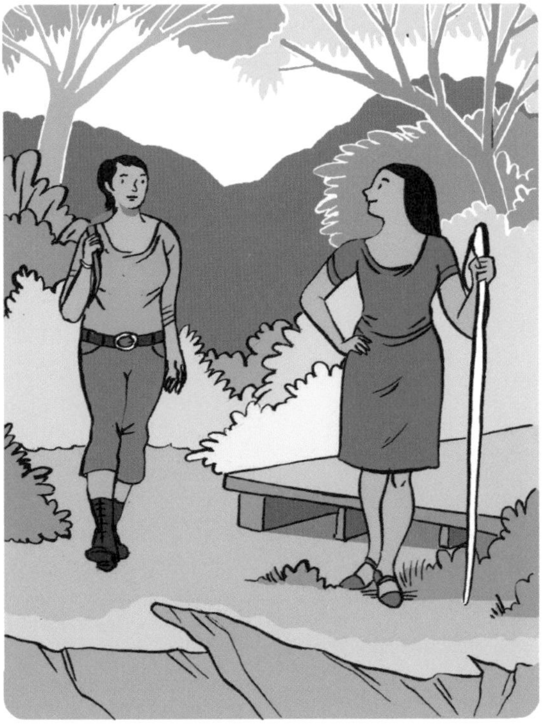
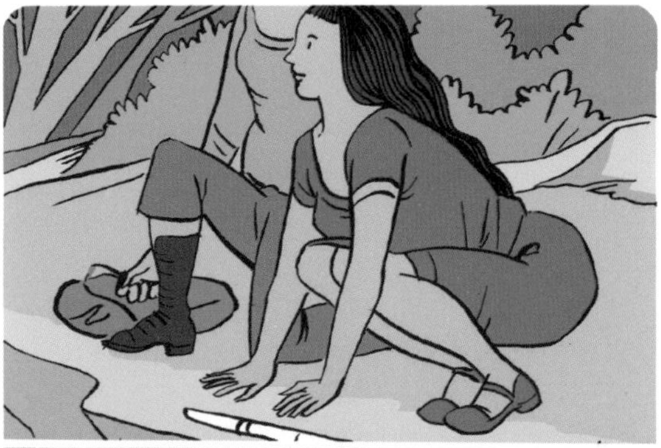
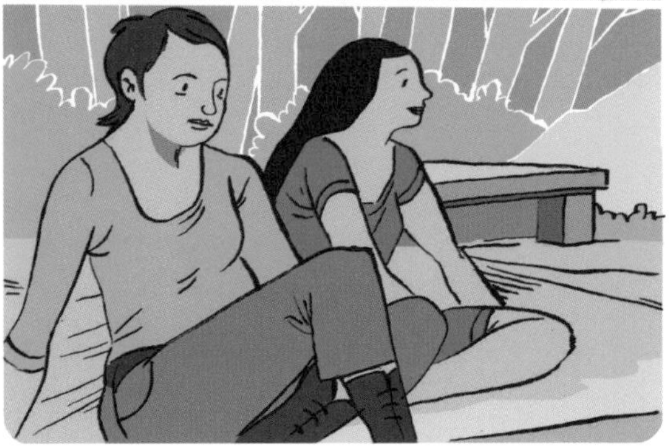

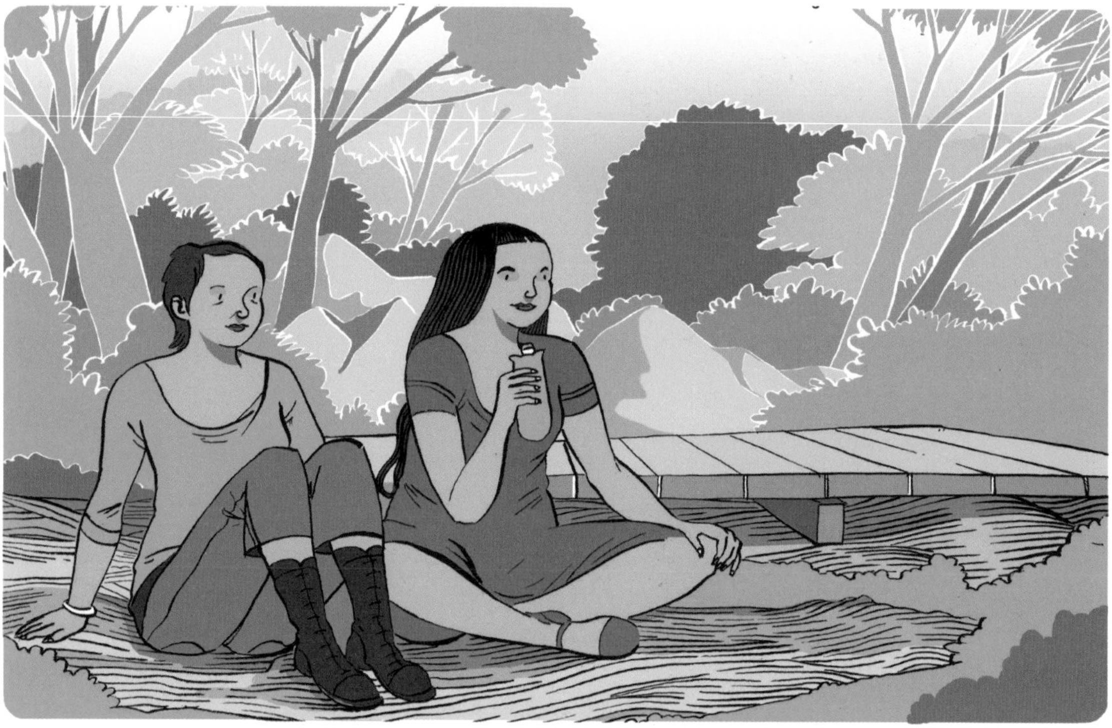

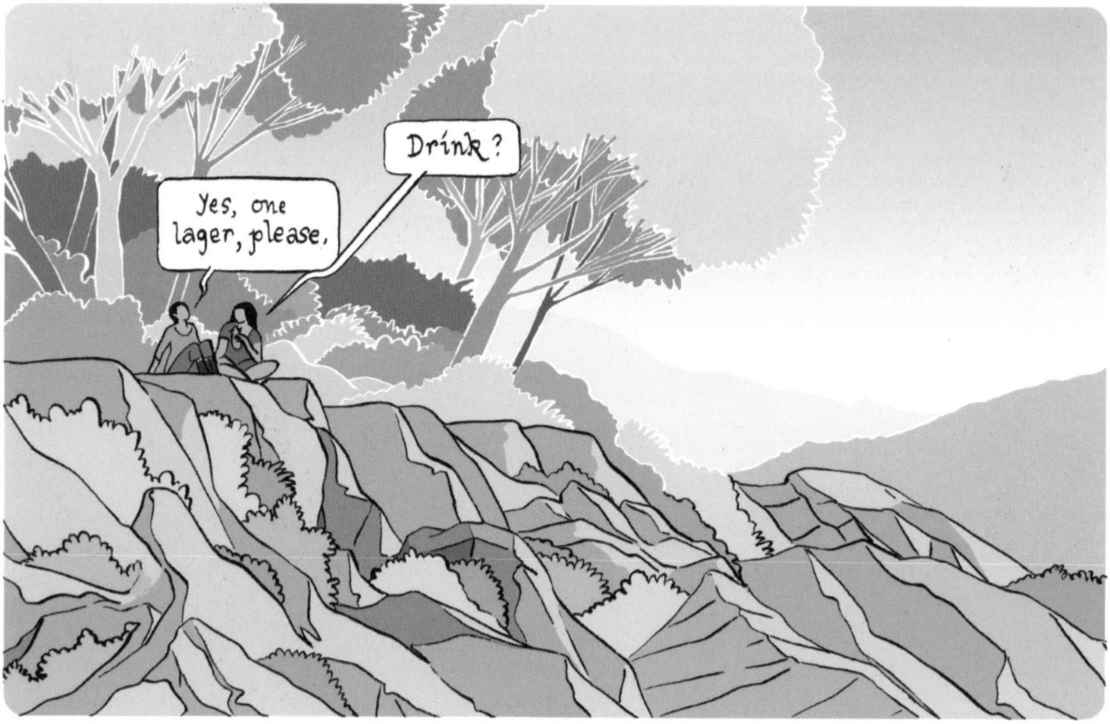
Drink?
Yes, one lager, please.

Oh, that was really scrummy... wait—what, how did you make the dal again?

It's just dal makhani with Beluga lentils instead of masoor dal.

"Beluga"? Like the whale? Wait — so, so they're not vegetarian?

Of course they're vegetarian — they're LENTILS!

OK, OK ...no need to get feisty.

You're the one getting feisty... not to mention a little wobbly.

Whatever! I'm on vacation, we're in the mountains, listening to *Loveless*, and having a Desi feast — how can one not drink?

I wasn't criticizing.

No, you were judging! You—you—you drink like, like... a fish! No, that's not right... like a bird! No, wait — that's, um, a...food-related idiom. Anyway... like a... incorporeal entity that, um, is also hydrophobic ... or something.

Now you've ceased to make any sense. And I'm sure I'm nothing like that.

Hoo boy, I really needed this break, you know? I was making myself loopy between drawing structural details and fretting about my non-existent book.

But it does exist, Anj... it's just not out in the wider world yet. The right publisher will come beating down your door, slavering like a wild beast to get their paws on your book, just you wait.

Yeah, I've BEEN waiting for years now! Where's my goddamn MacArthur genius grant?!

My goodness, you really are a project.

I'm just kidding! Jeez Louise!

Look, can't you take like two weeks off from your architecture gig? You need a breather. You could work on new stuff —

New stuff?! I've just spent the last two years plunging my heart into a 200-page magnum opus—

Just listen! You're clearly in a rut, fretting and sulking all the time... you just need some space to break out of that pattern.

I suppose. It's no good, Anj... you're stuck in a little echo chamber and you can't move forward.

I know. And honestly, it's like you enjoy feeling sorry for yourself sometimes. But all this wallowing is just holding you back.

Now wait a minute—

Not criticizing! I'm just offering an observation.

Still—

Don't be stubborn. Live outside your head for a spell.

I'll stock up on chicken and herring treats for Ampersand.

You're right.

Of course I'm right! I've got a goddamn Ph.D.!

Ha ha!

Not at all. What are astral twins for, if not for bullshit putting-upping?

You're a doll, Priya — honestly. Putting up with all my bullshit.

Well, it's nice to have someone who believes in me. I'm sure my parents would have been mortified if they knew I was sinking half my days into making comics ...

Your ma and baba were very proud of you when you did architecture and I'm sure they would have come round eventually to appreciating your new career.

Are you insane?! They were strictly old-school Bengalis!

Well, so are mine.

Well... we could adopt you.

What?

Nuh-uh! Somehow you lucked out with super-arty hipster Bengali parents so there's no comparison. If you were my sister, my dad would have been like, "What, beti? You are retreating to a mountain? You think you are a saddhu?"

We could adopt you, my poor orphan child.

You're so fucking sweet to me.

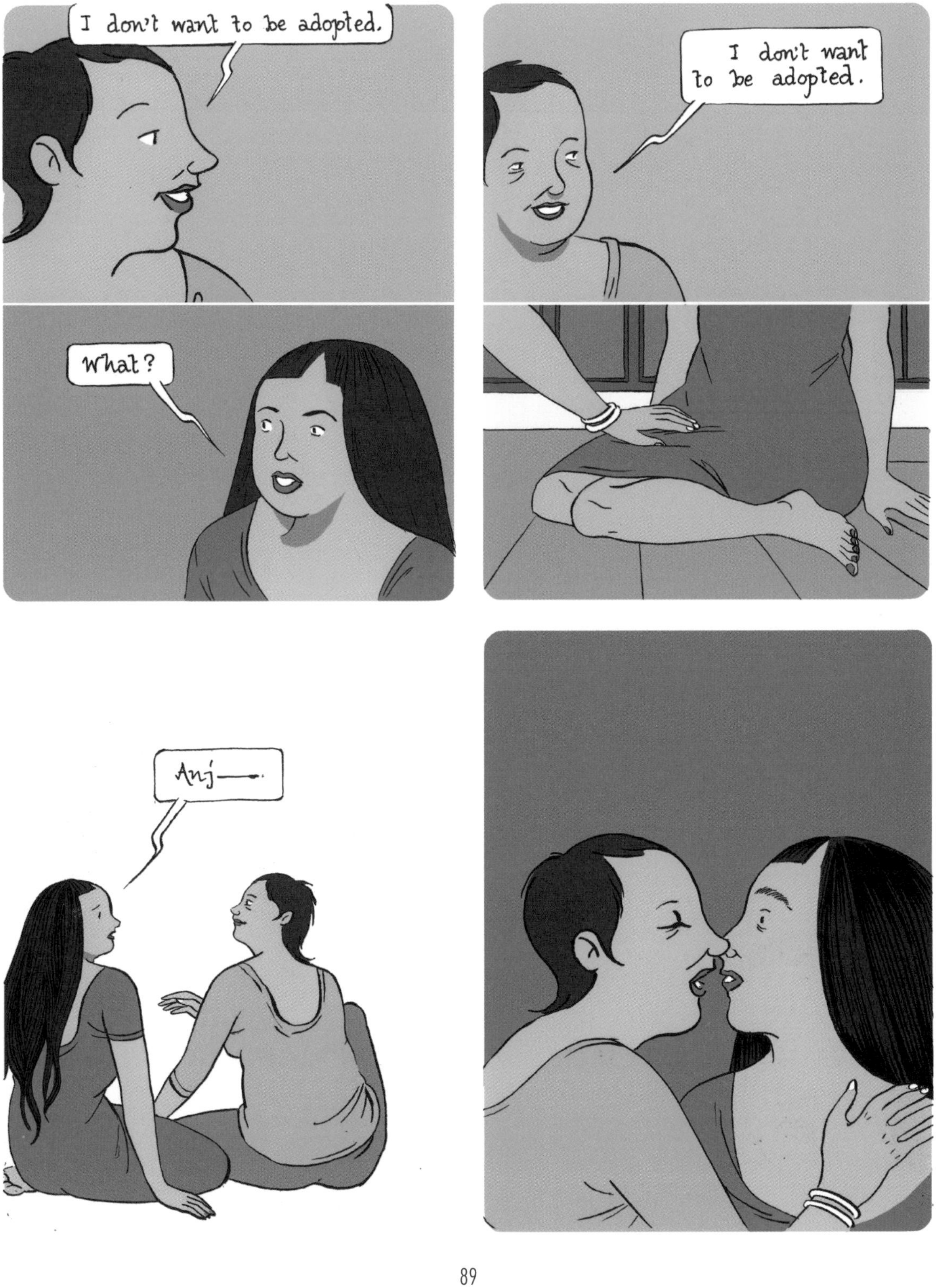
I don't want to be adopted.
I don't want to be adopted.
What?
Anj—.

Jesus, Anj! What's gotten into you?!

Oh, no.

D-don't you like me? I thought you—

Christ, Anj! I love you dearly... but you can't just —

But you broke up with Sheila, didn't—

That was only a month ago! And it doesn't mean I want to have a romantic encounter with my BEST FRIEND!

Jesus!

Priya — Just — let's both just clear our heads, shall we?

let's — let's just talk about this in the morning, OK? I'm — I'm gonna put these — these dishes in the sink.

OK?

OK.

Good.

You — you said you would woo me...

...with — with pakoras!

Noncommittal

Well, that was a disaster. What was I thinking? We drove to the train station the next morning, mainly in silence. Priya said "I love you, kiddo" or something equally noncommittal.

Is it that I'm attracted to anyone who's nice to me? Or was it all that wine? 20 more pages to paint, have to scan and clean up all pages... that's another... two months?

God, I swear she was flirting with me. How could I have read her so poorly?

Wooooooowwww

Oh, whatever. What the hell do I even want anyway? A girlfriend? A boyfriend? What a pain in the ass. Who needs it, Ampersand?

Not me.

Splurp Flurp

Oh, and I think I've been officially ghosted by Tina, so that's that, I guess.

Well, we've hit the five-month mark and I have eight pages of painted comics to show for it. Almost out of neutral gray paint though — a trip to the art supply store beckons.

I head to my favorite spot, a small hill overlooking the field just north of dog beach. Streams of teens in gym shorts run up and over the topography, terriers chase frisbees and hey! look — a hipster picnic.

It's not quite February temperatures. So I go out for a walk in Prospect Park. The massive family BBQs have long since dissipated. Now it's Park Slope dads with woolly caps and glasses, Prospect Heights moms who were once '90s punks.

Please use your indoor voice, Elijah.

POOPYPANTS!

I halfheartedly consider approaching the hairy 20-somethings and asking them if "the kids" have subcultures anymore, or if they're just in thrall to technology and corporate culture.

Dude, I'm literally, like, sorry not sorry

Brooklyn parrots flit by overhead.

Ok, only four more pages to paint now — I do believe we're in the home stretch.

OOF

Priya emailed to say she hoped we were still OK, I said yes, of course. Though I really want to just hide from her forever.

Keith, my old colleague from Chad's office, called to say he has some work for me, three or four days a week. I say yes as my funds are slowly dwindling.

The prospect of freelance dollars impels me to splurge on a bottle of Carmenere, spinach tortellini, and an artichoke for dinner.

I'm not sure that this fits into your dietary profile, darling.

snf snf

My drawing hand has seized up into a claw and my butt is throbbing but: 80 pages pencilled, inked, and now, painted. Next I have to scan and clean up the whole thing, but not today.

Instead, I go to Mr. Lee's to buy ingredients for vegetarian Korean tofu stew. I show Mr. Lee my previous attempt, which meets with some enthusiasm.

Ha ha ha! This is **not** Soondubu Jjigae!

Ha ha!

It's unusually warm so in the evening I go up to the roof to watch the sunset. There's a murmuration of starlings in the south, a mourning dove on the picnic table. Ingrid from 3R comes up for a glass of Zweigelt.

Hey, look! Mr. Muscles is out barbecuing again in his underwear!

Ooh! That's a lot of ... man.

After dinner, in thanks for allowing me to come this far with my book, I offer incense and fruit to Saraswati, goddess of music, art, and knowledge. Just like my mom used to do at home: one of the few times she would undo her braid or bun and let her hair down.

And now the somewhat tedious task of scanning all the finished pages and cleaning them up in Photoshop.

Oh, thank goddess for the clone stamp.

At the end of the day I have eight pages processed so it looks like another week of this digital massaging.

How much kibble can you possibly ingest?!

Woooowww

Today is Dad's birthday. I go out to the deli and buy 20 red roses which I sew into a garland to hang around his and Mom's photos.

Rakhi and I go out in the evening to Barbès, where a Romanian chanteuse is singing old folk songs and the occasional Tom Waits cover.

When I mentioned to Jyoti that I was ready to print mockups of the book, she said why don't I come over to her place and do it there — she has lots of ink for her printer and some time over the weekend.

Meow meow! Hey, babe!

I can hardly believe my good fortune to know someone so generous.

I bring over an external drive and we begin cranking out three copies of the book. She sets up batch printing so we take a breather and have some Indian takeout for lunch.

Where are my extra chilies, for god's sake?!

They probably thought you couldn't handle it.

They know I'm desi!

The printing goes on until evening, by which time we have broken into the Hefeweizen that Jyoti is partial to and — oh, look! A bottle of Tempranillo.

Oh! I say —

It's all yours, hon.

We are halfway done so I'll have to come back tomorrow to finish up but it has been a productive day, all told.

y-you are like, an amazing h-human person

Yes, dear.

After printing all the pages out, I assemble three mockups of the book to send out to the top three publishers on my wish list.

Oh, Ampersand! You always colonize the choicest territories!

I wrap each mockup in brown Kraft paper and enclose a carefully scripted cover letter in each. I sit down in front of Ma Saraswati and ask for her blessings.

The ladies at the post office on 9th Street are chirpy as I send my mockups off into the world.

Is there anything fragile or hazardous in these?

Um, no... they're just... comics?

Ooh, comics! I guess that could be potentially hazardous.

I feel some postpartum anxiety— an emptiness which looks wine bottle-shaped, somewhat tediously. Jyoti and I go out to the Otter & Trumpet for two drinks only.

You did it!

We did it!

But now what?

99

A little bit at sea after all these months of focusing on comics. Luckily I'm starting part-time architectural work at Keith's office next week so I'm not completely lost.

Mala's invited me to a party next week, which means I will get a chance to practice my social skills.

In the afternoon, I amble out to the art supply store — on my way back, in the terrace of The Gate, is Timo from high school. My first kiss.

Anjali?

I join him for a drink. He lives in Munich but is visiting NYC on a business trip.

You used to be... such a goth.

Oh, I guess I still am... just not... explicitly.

I tell Timo about my "career" in architecture and in comics, about my book.

So what are you doing now that you've sent it off?

Oh, just waiting, I suppose.

I show him some pages from the book.

Anj— these are great! But you can't just stop drawing—keep going!

Um, I'm not sure what to write about anymore, you know? I kind of blew it all on this book.

Just write anything! I don't know, why don't you keep a comics diary or something? Those are pretty popular, no?

What, like a memoir? I don't know ... maybe?

Timo is still tall, handsome, and genuinely sweet. I never ask him why he broke up with me but that's OK.

So guess what? I'm working part-time again. 20 hours a week at the architecture office I flirted with last year. Which means getting out of the house three times a week and a consequent sense of self-worth and purpose.

The work is fine and right up my alley — I'm drawing interior elevations and electrical plans for a couple of residential projects. Couldn't be easier.

Anjali, are you using the pen file settings I mentioned?

Uh, no... I can't find them on the server.

I put a lot of effort into those, you know.

I treat myself to a lunch of samosa chaat and dive happily into the middle-class throng, the gainfully employed at midday leisure in Bryant Park.

I, like, literally died!

OH. MY. GOD. You must have been, like, totally impacted!

Yes well, you see — The only problem is that this is _my_ lunch.

A full eight hours of paying work accomplished — I deserve a reward. And so: I gleefully purchase a $13 (!) bottle of Garnacha instead of the usual $8 plonk. Cheers to the work-force — the goddamn backbone of this beautiful country!

FUCK! Why won't anyone publish my graphic novel, Ampersand? Oh, right — because the world just won't be able to withstand the ferocity of my artistic genius, that's why.

SIGH

Goddamnit! Where the fuck is Mala? She said she'd be here at 10:00!

Maybe I'll head to the bedroom where it's quieter.

It's like a totally organic artisanal pig farm and we have so much love for the little ones—

OOF!

Even as you're SLAUGHTERING THEM?!

OH, MY. GOD. I was like OBSESSED with that Donna Tartt book — *The Goldfish?*

I, like, literally lost my shit!

Yikes! I've got to get out of this scrum!

So I was, like, yeah, I'm a do five Aperol Spritzes...

I would love to get to, like, 5,000 followers!

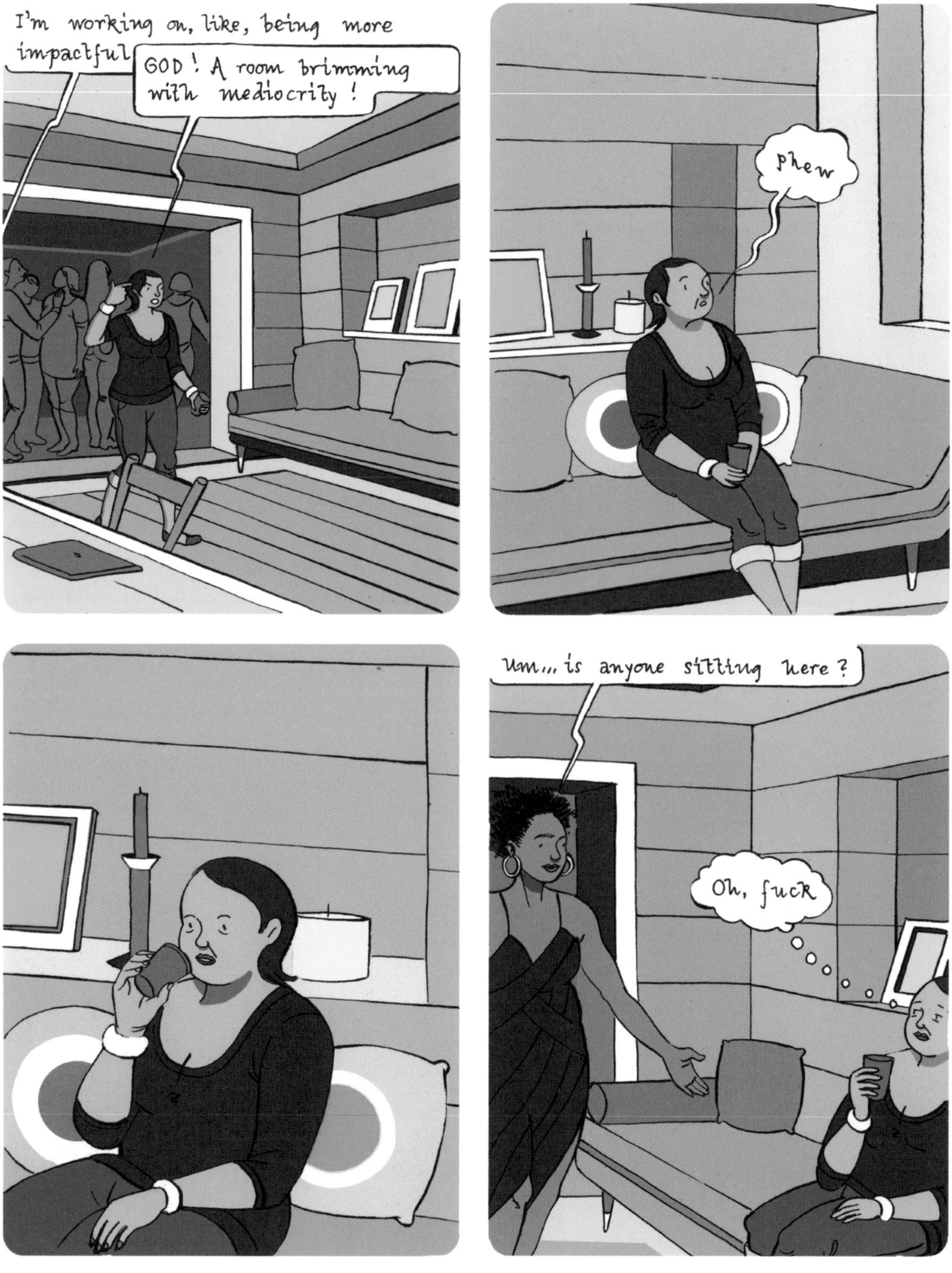
I'm working on, like, being more impactful
GOD! A room brimming with mediocrity!
phew
Um... is anyone sitting here?
Oh, fuck

Um, no... please. Have — have a seat.

Oh, my god, thanks— my friend Mamie invited me here but she's running late and I don't know ANY of these people.

Oh! I'm — I'm in the same situation, actually... I've been somewhat... ditched, I think.

Ugh... sorry to hear that, hon. But at least you're not the only trans person in an apartment full of cis folks.

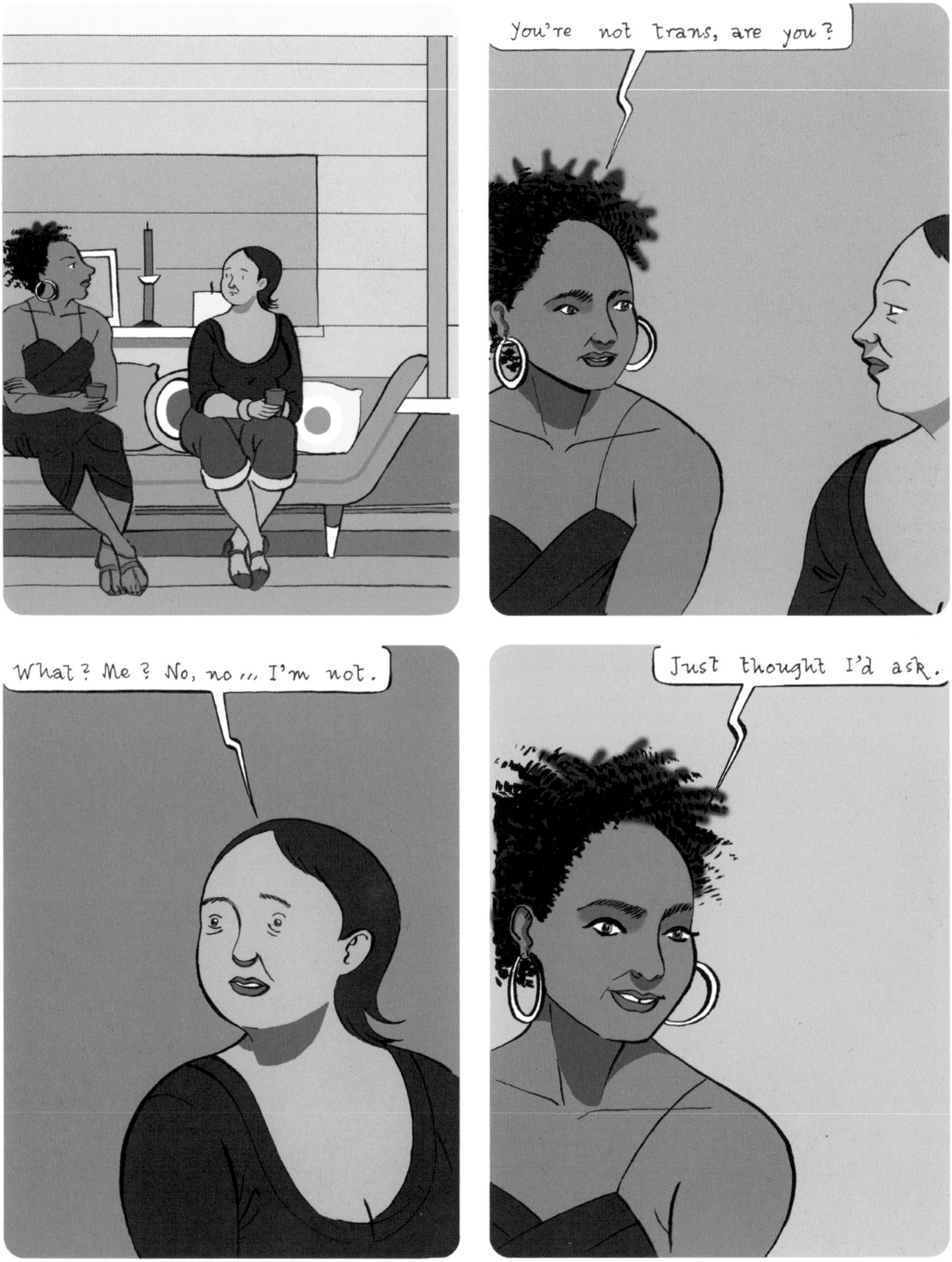
You're not trans, are you?
What? Me? No, no ... I'm not.
Just thought I'd ask.

My name's Titania, by the way.

Ooh! Um.... the faerie queen.

Yeah, that's right. Most people don't even realize they're in the presence of royalty!

Well, I'm pleased to make your acquaintance, your highness. I'm Anjali.

Hmm.... "light"? "Angel"? No.... "offering," right?

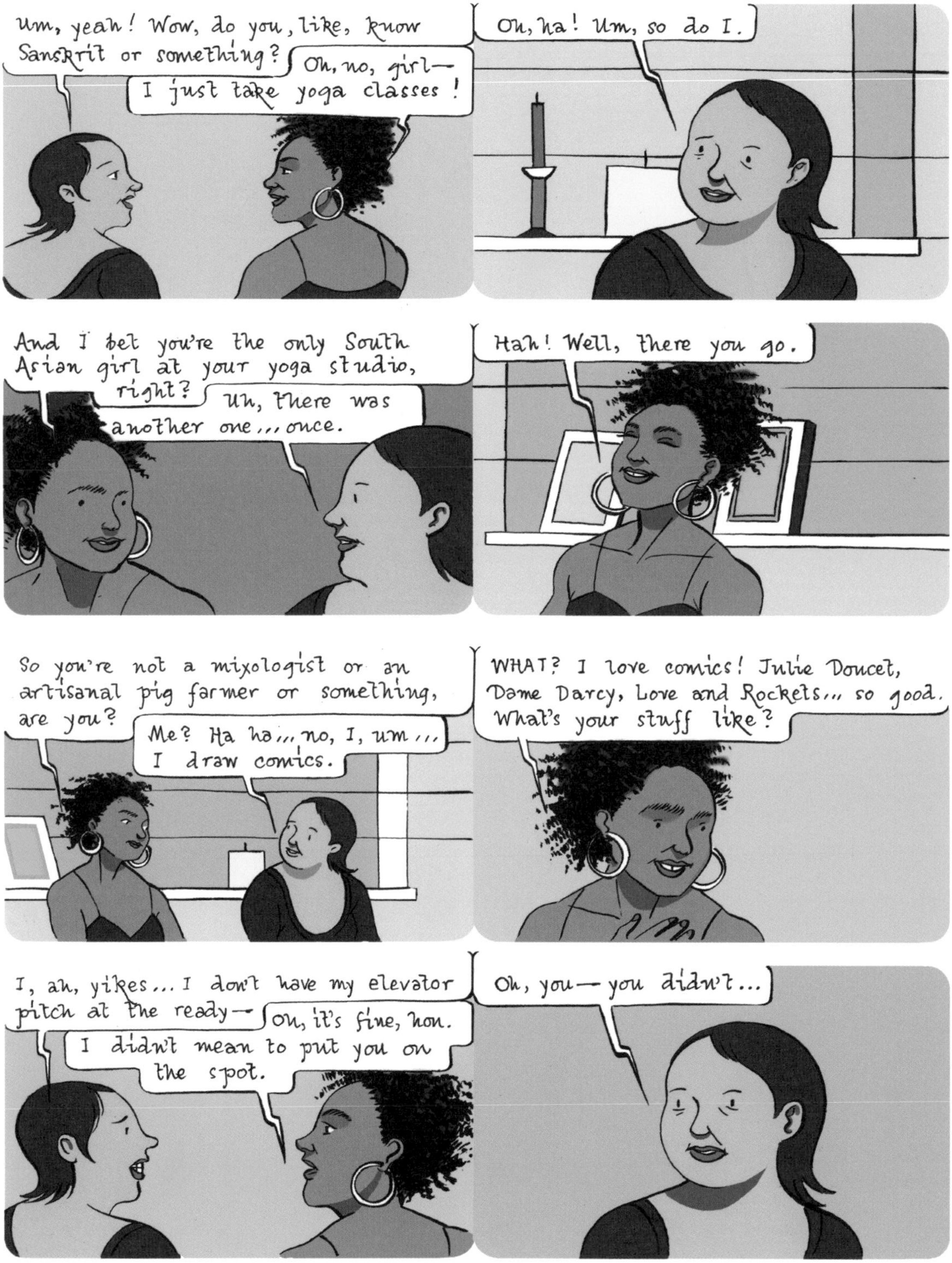
Um, yeah! Wow, do you, like, know Sanskrit or something?
Oh, no, girl— I just take yoga classes!
Oh, ha! Um, so do I.
And I bet you're the only South Asian girl at your yoga studio, right?
Uh, there was another one... once.
Hah! Well, there you go.
So you're not a mixologist or an artisanal pig farmer or something, are you?
Me? Ha ha... no, I, um... I draw comics.
WHAT? I love comics! Julie Doucet, Dame Darcy, Love and Rockets... so good. What's your stuff like?
I, ah, yikes... I don't have my elevator pitch at the ready—
Oh, it's fine, hon. I didn't mean to put you on the spot.
Oh, you— you didn't...

Well, I'd love to see your work some time.

I—I'd be happy to show you.

What—what do you—

There you are, girl! I was stuck in the kitchen, talking to some douchey finance bro.

Um, yeah, Mamie... you were supposed to be here, like, AN HOUR AND A HALF AGO!

I know! I'm sorry! The G train was like, mad fucked up! There was some crazy shuttle bus action at Bedford-Nostrand...

It's fine, it's fine. Miss Anjali here was giving me the offering of her company in your absence.

Oh, hi.

Anjali, Mamie.

Hi Anjali! Thanks for taking care of Titania!

Oh, it's a pleasure. She's saved me from having to deal with those awful people out there—

Hey! Those are friends of mine!

Oh no! I didn't mean....

Ha ha! It's OK... I only really know the host. The rest are pretty horrid, to be sure.

So WHY would you invite me in the first place?!

I wanted to see you!

You can see me anyti—

OMG Mamie! I, like, love your haircut!

OK, we have to let everyone see how cute we look tonight!

You maybe wanna get out of here?

Oh, hell, yes.

It's been a month now since I sent my book off to publishers. Only one has responded, asking if I would consider doing a digital, serialized version of it.

I tell them no.

Titania texted. After we ditched the party we went out for a drink and chatted until 2:00 in the morning.

We're supposed to get together Thursday next week. I'm glad she's a drinker like me and not into "meeting up for coffee."

Ampersand sleeps with his feet splayed against the baseboard because it's 90 degrees out at night.

That can't be very comfortable, sweetie.

So after several weeks of inactivity, I've got a new freelance gig. I'm working at a small office in Tribeca, helping out my old colleague Keith with renovating an upper east side townhouse.

The work so far is easy-peasy: interior elevations, staircase drawings, bathroom plans. There's four other people in my wing of the studio— (I'm the only girl)—most notably Gerald, a beardy dude who seems to have phlegmy wads perpetually caught in his respiratory tract.

> uhhhhnnnn—!
> :HRRK:

It's nice to get out of the house on a regular basis again though of course I have forgotten, during my hibernation, how annoying other people are.

> Why is every single person on this train playing this *fucking* fruit game?!

Note to self: must master further meditation techniques.

So #blessed to be getting paychecks again. I splurge on a $16 Malbec to go with dinner: fried bitter melon, dal, and leftover biryani. Ampersand gets an extra whitefish treat at bedtime.

> Scrummy, right? Now do you promise not to harass me at 2:00 in the morning?

> smack slor

At the office, I check my emails only to find out that two months after sending mockups to my top three publishers, the other two have weighed in and said no. Both on the same day.

Oh, no

And, to think that I went into this with so much confidence.

I must have groaned or something because Bertrand, who sits next to me, asks me what's wrong. I tell him and he kindly offers words of solace.

You just gotta keep at it, chica.

I walk around Battery Park City during lunch in a bit of a daze.

I cannot even be bothered with making dinner. I heat up a tin of peas in some mustard oil and nigella seeds and watch old episodes of *Deep Space Nine*.

Cardassian rule may have been oppressive but at least it was simple,

It's all coming crashing down, sweetie.

Saturday 10:00 a.m., yoga—we attempt flying pigeon pose to crow, which I manage by some miracle. I'll take any miracles — tiny, tiny ones — at this point.

YIKES!

My cauliflower stem-leaf curry has thoroughly lost its appeal. I wonder if even Madhur Jaffrey could make these leavings taste like anything other than roughage.

UGH! Time for some new austerity-measure recipes.

I unload my woes to Vinita, whose book of poetry has just come out. She comes up with a list of smaller publishers that she thinks would like my work. I promise her that I will send them PDFs of the book.

I'm so happy for you, V! Pass some of that poetic magic my way, won't you?

Of course, Sakhi.

That evening, I hear a Jacques Brel song at the Otter & Trumpet and it reminds me of Madame Cuvélier, whose swagger and confidence I wish I could tap into.

114

Working on bathroom drawings. The client has picked out a clamshell-motif sink and a fish-shaped spout for the powder room.

Hey, Anjali—do you still—*uhhhnnn!*—like, have cousins and stuff in India?

Uh, yeah... why?

I feel like I've become the go-to girl for when the mega-rich need help envisioning their shitters.

So—*uuhhnnn!*—don't take this the wrong way, but do any of them do, like, cheap Auto-CAD drafting? Or do they—*uuhnn*—all, like, work in call centers?

I wish my own bathroom wasn't so vile. Short of immersing the entire room in a bath of hydrochloric acid, there's no way of getting rid of the black mold that covers every tiled surface.

Bring me more Rioja, beardy white peon! And take some cough drops, for Goddess's sake!

Y-y-y-yes, Maharani.

Oh, well. Maybe one day when I'm fabulously wealthy from **MAKING COMICS**, I can design my own loo, with gold-leaf *putti* adorning the ceiling and a toilet modelled after the Papal throne.

Yeah, no... none of them are doing any of those things, **actually**.

Oh god, what a fucking fool

Summertime

It's so hot today. So hot I don't want to get out of bed and so hot I can't manage to stay in bed.

Subrata emails me asking how I'm doing. I'm too ashamed to tell her that no one has been interested in the book so far.

Godamnit.

I halfheartedly work on some small paintings, ideas I've been nursing for a while, images that wouldn't fit into comics.

To what end?

In the evening I send PDFs of the book to the five smaller publishers that Vinita suggested. I do this with little enthusiasm.

I'm trying, Ampersand… I'm trying.

Work continues apace. Jeremy, the associate partner, tells me that Keith likes my work and finds me pleasant to work with and would I consider a full-time position? I tell him no, thank you, I value my freedom.

During lunch (saag, dal, chana masala) I notice that Paolo is using Google maps to wander up and down the virtual aisles of... a CVS?... in Boca Raton?

I didn't even know you could do that. Also, now I'm a little scared of Paolo.

I thank Goddess I have a short commute to and from Park Slope. I cannot take much more of this humanity. Wake up! Look up from your fucking screens! This fascist regime has made you all morons! Fucking lemmings!

Dinner is a baked tempeh, spinach, and tomato casserole, accompanied by a peppery syrah. Ampersand has resumed his endearing habit of knocking items off the end table to capture my attention in the small hours.

Drawing elevations of one of three (!) kitchens in this townhouse project which means doing online research for canapé warmers. What are canapés anyway? Have I ever had one?

Ooh, I say — the spinach ones are quite exquisite.

Rah-ther.

WOW

Titania has suggested a Cuban place for drinks tonight. Just getting her text helps me over the mid-afternoon work hump. I resolve not to moan to her about my publication and rejection woes.

We meet up at 7:00 pm. Titania's wearing a Swans T-shirt and orders a Cuba Libre. I get a Mayabe beer.

Ah! I used to love *The Burning World* — my mom thought it sounded like they were chanting in Sanskrit!

So she was a goth at heart too.

I invite Titania over for a Bengali dinner next week. She's never had bitter melon or *Begun Bhaja* or *Alur Dom*. I haven't made a meal for anyone else in ages.

Bibimbap

I don't know, Chrissy— I'm doing ok but I feel kind of *stuck*, you know? Most of these publishers won't respond to my book, and some have just straight up said no. I- I just invested so much in trying to make this graphic novel thing work— I can't — I can't just <u>try again</u>, you know?

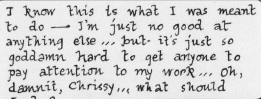

I know this is what I was meant to do — I'm just no good at anything else ... but it's just so goddamn hard to get anyone to pay attention to my work ... Oh, damnit, Chrissy ... what should I do?

Are you even listening to me?

Just instagramming my Bibimbap ... keep talkin', Babe.

119

I've gotten bitter melons and parvals from little India. I use Dad's recipe for khichuri which includes peas and potatoes along with the rice and lentils. I throw in some tomatoes too.

It's just chemistry, Ampersand!

Titania brings over some blueberries and green tea ice cream.

Well, hello there, young master!

Oooh, I love your hair, Titania!

I put on some Dead Can Dance before dinner and we snack on papadums.

I needed this... the F train was stuck between 2nd avenue and Delancey for, like, twenty minutes and that was not fun.

Titania works at the Immigration Defense Project. At the moment, she's working with an artist on an illustrated book about how to deal with the cops and ICE if they come for you.

I can't believe you had to go to work today.

Oh, it's OK ... at least I had something to look forward to afterward.

Eventually we sit down to dinner.

Ooh, I like these neem leaves.

Yeah, they're a little too much on their own but perfect with some fried eggplant.

So you learned to cook from your folks, huh?

Pretty much. They were always talking about food when they weren't busy cooking it so I guess I just absorbed all that.

Ha ha... my mom was like that too, especially when it came to seafood.

Noooooo! Oh, lordy, the never-ending fish dialogues!

Truth! Me, I'd rather discuss vegetables.

Oh, yes! Speak my language!

Mmmm... what did you say these are called?

Parvals. Or potols, as we say in Bengali. In a poppy seed and mustard sauce.

Sooo good!

Aww, I'm so happy you like it.

More wine?

Oh, definitely.

Woo0o0oooWw

Oh, that's lovely — thank you, hon.

Oh, you betcha!

Girl, why are you suddenly channeling Sarah Palin?!

Ha ha ha! Oh, no! What's happening to me?

Don't you be goin' rogue on me now.

Ha ha! Yer darn tootin'!

Ha ha... oh, dear! Oh, have some more dal, won't you?

Thank you, hon.

Mmmm... my mom used to make a lentil soup but it wasn't as good as this.

Does — does your mom still like to cook?

Oh, we don't really talk anymore. Not since I transitioned.

Oh, I'm sorry...

It's all good, hon. I have my other families.

Anyway, who needs family like that? Acting like coming out is on the same level as, like, admitting you're a serial killer or something.

Did you ever have to have — that kind of conversation with your folks?

Ah, me? Um, no,,, I...we just never talked about ... about that kind of stuff.

Uh-huh.

Was there anything you wish you could have told them?

I, uh,,, I'm not sure. I,,, I don't even know myself.

I'm sorry, hon. I don't mean to put you on the spot.

You — you didn't

We can talk about something else.

No, no ,,, it's just —

Can I have some more chutney?

Oh, yeah,,, of course.

Mmmm... I love this! Sweet and sour mango, huh? What did you call it?

It's — it's called "Tok."

Yum. Your folks taught you well, young Jedi.

I — I'm sure they would have appreciated hearing that.

Well, it might have been *interesting* to meet them. Though I'm not sure what they would have thought of me.

Ummm... yeah. They were conservative in a very... very Indian way.

Well, hello there, young master.

WOW

Ah! What's all this?

I....

I - I guess now... now... there might be a few things I wish I could share with them.

Well... why don't you share them with me?

I— I'm not sure what's happening to me. I am bewitched, entranced. There are aspects of myself that are starting to come into focus and other facets which are becoming blurry, softer.

There is an alchemy at work, a sparkling transmutation. Like muscle and bone turned to light and air. There are moments when I am unencumbered by my body.

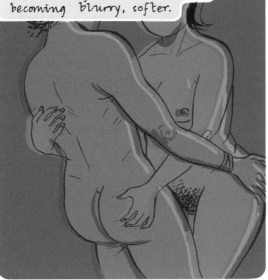

Like weights that have dropped, ballast that has been jettisoned.

This is witchery of the sweetest kind. I'm enrapt, spellbound. Like we've written and cast a mutual spell over ourselves.

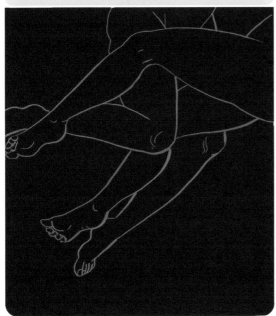

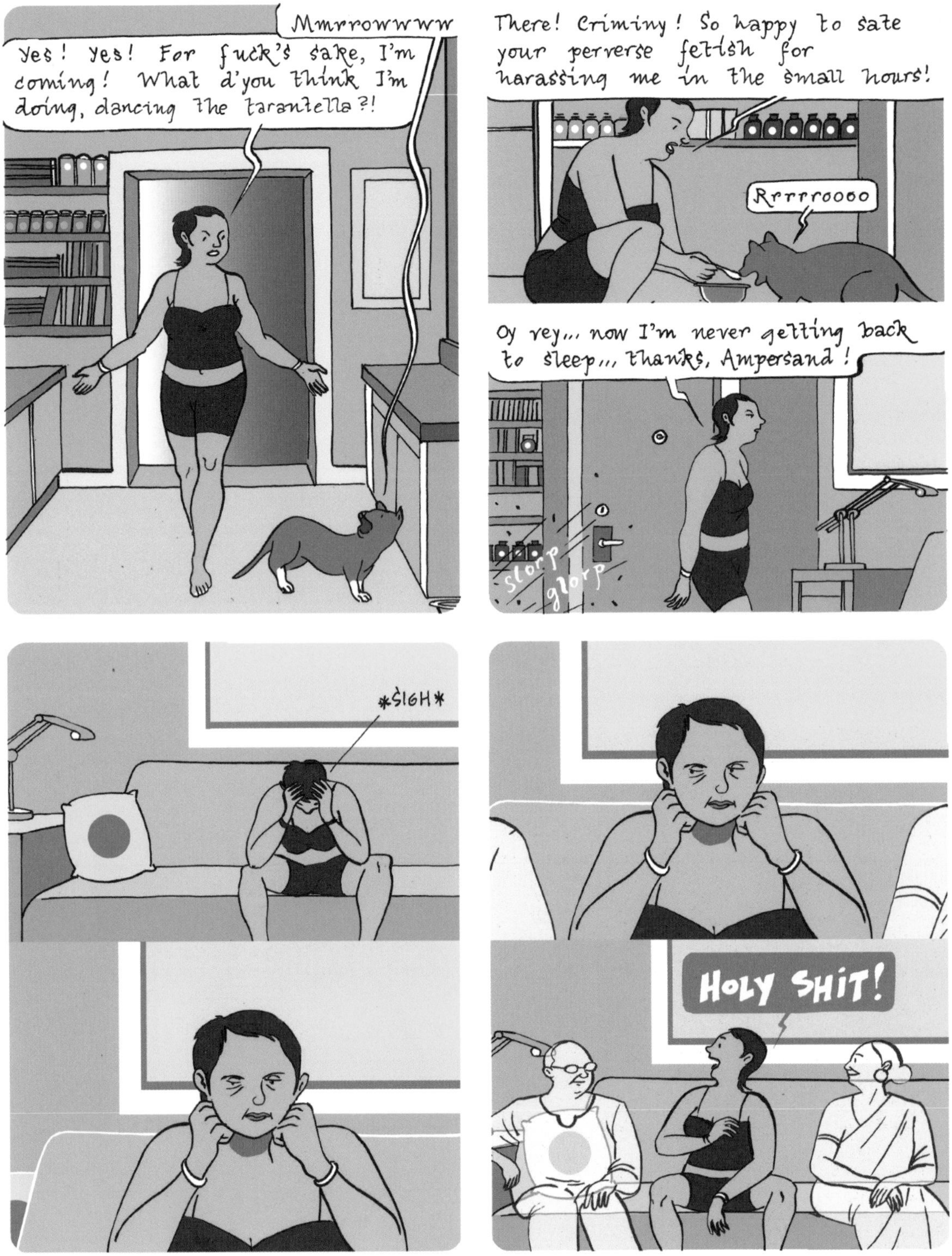
Mmrrowwww
Yes! Yes! For fuck's sake, I'm coming! What d'you think I'm doing, dancing the tarantella?!
There! Criminy! So happy to sate your perverse fetish for harassing me in the small hours!
Rrrrroooo
Oy vey... now I'm never getting back to sleep... thanks, Ampersand!
slorp glorp
SIGH
HOLY SHIT!

Oof, beti—what bad language.

Ma?! What—?

Hello, beti.

Baba?! Oh, my god, am I dreaming—?

Na re, Anju ... you're awake! Remember, your cat just woke you up, na?

Yes but ... oh, god! Shouldn't you guys be, um ... reincarnated or something by now?

Oh, beti ... it's more complicated than that, Lord Krishna will explain it to you himself one day.

Uuuhhh ... this is all really really weird.

Oh, shonamoni ... aren't you glad to see us?

Well, yeah ... of course ... **BUT YOU'RE DEAD!!**

Oof, so blunt!

Anyway, Anju ... we just came to check up on you.

Y-y-you did?

Of course, darling... especially now with that nasty orange clown-faced buffoon in the White House, we thought you'd need some... parental guidance.

You're here... because of... Trump?

Chhi chhi! Don't say his name! Anyway, don't worry — he won't be around much longer. Something to do with... Russian flying squirrel drones?

Oof! She's not supposed to know these things! Anyway, beti... it will be ok. What else was there...? Oh, yes! Don't give up on your book! Most of these publishers are idiots. Fortunately, there is one who has taste.

!

We don't have much time, baby... tell us, the part-time architecture is working out for you?

Umm... yeah, I guess... except for this guy with the throat problem...

Oh, go easy on him, Anju! Anyway, there is one last thing...

Ummm... what?

WHEN ARE YOU GOING TO FIND A NICE INDIAN BOY AND GET MARRIED YAAR?!

HA HA HA!

Just kidding beti! You go out and find a nice girl, na?

"A nice girl?" Wait, what—?

Oh, Anjali! For goodness' sake, we're _dead_! You don't have to pretend with _us_ anymore!

Anyway, sweetie... we have to go now. But... just one last thing.

W-w-what?

MAKE SURE SHE'S BENGALI!!

Oh, no...

Ma? Baba?

R-r-russian flying squirrel drones?

Rooooooo....

Wow, Anj... she sounds really rad. How serious do you think this is?

I — I don't know, Priya.

Well, when are you going to see her again?

Um we have plans to hang out next week. She — she's visiting friends in Woodstock or something now.

Hmmm, I'm sensing something out of the ordinary here.

You don't say.

What — what's wrong? Oh, my god— nothing.

Are you still upset about that night — in the Adirondacks?

YOU'RE the one who got upset!

Oh, Anj...

132

You mean the world to me. I think you're lovely and sweet and amazing and I love spending time with you and we've been friends for so long — why would we want to fuck all that up?

No, you're right. I — I didn't know what I wanted anyway. I — I was just drunk.

Anj, Titania sounds like an amazing girl. I know you are gonna be great for each other. I mean, look at you! You're already glowing! Like, in a really gothy sort of way. How you used to look!

I've always been this way.

Oh, Priya....

Last day at Keith's office, now that the drawings I've been working on have been submitted to the landmarks committee. I hand in my final timesheet.

Leaving us so soon?

Not by choice, I assure you.

Keith says they may have work later in the year, but not until they get approval and permits from the city for this townhouse project.

Well, in the meantime, good luck with your doodles... or, what do you call them?

Huhhhkkk

COMICS!

I go home and make a barley salad (sundried tomatoes, pine nuts, bamboo shoots) for dinner.

Damnit. What the hell do I do now? Should I go hunting for another freelance gig? What is my goddamn trajectory?

Oh, Ampersand... I can't go back to a full-time job with yet another toxic boss-man. I - I'm just not interested in architecture any more, anyway. And— and I really love drawing comics. I'm— I'm good at it ...

even if none of these publishers think so.

God, at least when I quit Chad's office I had some sort of road map, even if it was tattered, smudged, and only partially legible.

And I certainly had no signposts to mark the way into affairs of the heart. I usually have such intense daily contempt for other people, it's jarring to feel some warmth and affection toward *one* girl.

WooWoWr

I'm sorry, didn't we JUST have dinner? Like half an hour ago?

Working at home has turned me into a sad little hermitess. And Titania... was that a fluke? I—I don't know what's happening.

Before I go to bed, I ask Ma Saraswati for guidance. Divine Mother, please light the way for me. I promise to stop being such a lush.

Maybe it's time for a do-over. For a start, maybe I could move to Canada or the Netherlands, somewhere with national health care. So I wouldn't have to shell out over $500 a month to some corporate entity just to get asthma meds.

Sixteen puffs left... if I skip every other day, I can make this last a month...

The Dutch love comics, don't they?

Or I could move to India, to cultivate a connection to — well, anything, really — culture, family, history, some nebulous feeling, some sense of belonging that I've never had.

Ah, Anju! Why don't you come for tea and sweets this afternoon, yaar?

Nostalgic for a past that never existed.

I could become a sanyasini and sit in single-minded contemplation of the divine on a hill in Assam. Then I remember how miserable I am in hot weather. Could... really go for... even... a fuckin'... Rolling Rock... right now...

I should text Titania but I don't want yet again to appear overeager. So I don't. Even though I'm no good at playing it cool.

I wonder what she's up to this weekend.

Talked to Amalia on the phone in the morning. I love her to bits but she still seems ever so oblivious.

Mom says she would be up for having you home for Thanksgiving. If that's something you'd want.

GIVE ME STRENGTH

I spend a little time going over some Dolzauer études and then play along to a Nina Simone album.

Annalisa's yin yoga class in the afternoon. Mark the grunting topless dude is in attendance again, much to pretty much everyone's dismay.

Uunngh

In the evening I meet Oxana at Genre Reassignment at Branded Saloon. She reads some of her newer "fluffy" poems. Jeanne, Cat, and Briana are there too.

What's her name, this Indian girl?

Anjali. She seems a little bit at sea but... I don't know, I like her a lot.

Twilight

You wonder what all that education was for. Structures, materials, history, theory — Palladio, Hilberseimer, Le Corbusier, Brunelleschi — enfilade, parti, gesamtkunstwerk, dasein

And all I'm good at is drawing.

Well, I guess I had to at least TRY with this graphic novel crap. At least I made an effort. Otherwise I would have regretted it into my twilight years.

But now what? I'm too old and indifferent to architecture to keep doing that. I had it easy at Keith's office — better the devil you know and all that — but even that work was, well, meaningless.

At night Ampersand deigns to cuddle with me in bed even though it's warm. I'm reading Jane Eyre and feeling — oh, you know this by now — sorry for myself. Yes, I know — get over it.

9:00 a.m., yoga takes me away from myself, if only for a little while.

I find some extra 300 lb Arches watercolor paper in my stash, and start on a series of small paintings.

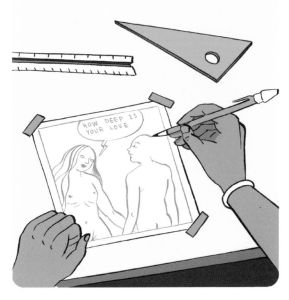

Late afternoon in Prospect Park: no dogs at dog beach so the ducks have it all to themselves.

The sweetness has been sucked out of sleep lately — but still, I just want to retreat.

Hey, you.

Hey hey.

How—how was your day?

Oh, fine. We had a big meeting with the mayor's office that went better than expected.

Oh, yeah, you said you were getting ready for that last week.

Uh-huh. Oh, and after that we all had chocolate cake for Nina's birthday. She's, like, 25 now.

Ooh, just a baby.

How 'bout you, hon? What did you get up to?

Oh, I sent my résumé out in the morning to an architectural consulting firm to see if I can't get some freelance work—

Um, then I worked on some art—like small paintings that are the size of 7-inch singles that are, like, inspired by actual singles.

Ooh, delicious... can you do "Cities in Dust"?

I will do that especially for you.

Um, then I went out to the pet store to get some more chicken and herring "pâté" for Ampersand.

I'm sure he'll be very grateful to you for that.

Oh, he won't. He only ever complains.

Oh, come now. Isn't he snuggling with you in bed?

He is... but either he's being affectionate, or, more likely, I make a good heat source on chilly Autumn nights.

I'm sure you do! My Angelina only deigns to lay herself down on my pelvis, which means I'm stuck on my back and cannot turn over for hours.

Awww. Nice to have a kitty-weight on you for a little while though.

What else?

Oh, I dunno. Just another ... hermity day really.

Hey, you OK?

Yeah, yeah! I'm— I'm good. I—in fact, I'm doing great.

Oh?

Um, yeah... well, the thing is, I got an email...

AND?

Well, it was from this small publisher...

WHAT?

Yeah, they, um... they want to meet with me... about the book.

Girl, you did it!

Oh, no... not yet, they haven't—

Shut the fuck up! You frickin' did it!

I...

Ah... I, um...

Yes?

The thing is, they're in Boston...

Uh huh.

143

And... well, they wanted to know if I could go up there, to their office, to talk about the book... and I was thinking, sure, might be nice to revisit Cambridge and such.

Make it a little vacation, you know? Maybe spend the weekend in Provincetown or something? I— I hate the beach normally but I was thinking it might be nice, with—with the Autumn chill and all...

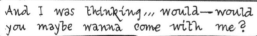

And I was thinking... would—would you maybe wanna come with me?

Oh hell yes.

Oh! Are you done? Well, thanks for slogging through all that. Sorry about all the self-pity.

But maybe you now have a sense, if a somewhat refracted version, of some of my experiences. As for that refraction: why filter these recollections through Anjali?

Well, if you'll forgive yet another digression, let me weave a few threads together here: like Anjali, I also met a trans girl at a party, sometime in 2016. We hit it off and stayed in touch.

I don't remember when we discussed the matter specifically but at some point she opened up to me the possibility that I was like her— that I was also trans.

I was, at my advanced age of 48, sadly unaware about a lot of trans issues. I didn't know about the broad spectrum of trans identities. Still unsure of what I was... I dipped a toe into trans waters and started using gender-neutral pronouns.

This eventually gave way and as most strangers had started to do anyway, used feminine (she/her/hers) pronouns for myself instead.

So! Can I get some drinks for you ladies tonight?

I trepidatiously started using the women's room when we went out, after several frightening episodes of being chased out of men's rooms. Thank goddess, the ladies never once harassed me.

More and more, I started to be recognized and affirmed as a woman.

You know, you seem like a very special lady.

DAAAAAAAAD SHUT UP!

So yeah, after half a century (I KNOW! I'm a late bloomer!) of being at sea, I finally kind of know who I am.

Which again brings me back to this book: maybe I should have realized that replacing myself with Anjali meant much more than I understood at the time.

That all the femme/women protagonists in my comics were telling me something.

That their voices were beckoning me, announcing that I was one of them.

yaaaassssss Queeeeeeenn

I started this comic as a "displaced memoir" (as my friend Adam called it) but soon it started growing other narrative tendrils, as Anjali started to divide herself from me.

So, dear reader — that's the general arc of it. Anjali began as a substitute but she's become her own —

I'm sorry... were you talking about ME?!

Whoa! Anj — what, ah... what are you doing here?

Oh, I was just out with Sneha and we espied you here, pontificating.

Umm... ha ha

I — I, ah, was just telling our dear reader here about the roots and, uh... blossoms... of this book.

Aha haaa... "blossoms"! So poetic yaar!

Uhhhh...

And what do you think of all this poesy, dear reader?

Well, they've only just finished th—

CHOOP!

148

I was addressing *th_em*, Miss Rajkumari ji, not you!

Ok, ok... I'll shut up now.

Oh yum! Is this the Rioja?

-sigh- Where's Titania when you need her?

"Substitute," huh?

I—

Hush. Anjali—c'est MOI.

She's such a diva.

Fin

After all that drama, it's time for...

COOKING WITH ANJALI & AMPERSAND
STARRING : *Baba's Khichuri* ★

1 Toast ¼ cup of yellow lentils (moong dal) & ¼ cup of red lentils (masoor dal) in a saucepan over medium heat for 3 minutes.

Transfer to into a bowl and set aside.

2 Heat 2 tsp. mustard oil in the saucepan & add 2 bay leaves, 3 cloves, 3 cardamom pods (split slightly,) 1 cinnamon stick & a 1" thumb of ginger, grated.

Fry for one minute.

3 Add the lentils & ½ cup of washed Basmati rice and sauté for a minute.
Introduce 1 tsp. ground cumin,
  ¼ tsp. ground turmeric,
  ¼ tsp. cayenne pepper, & 1 tsp. salt.
Fry for 3 minutes, stirring often.

Throw in 2½ cups of water and bring to a boil.

Meanwhile,

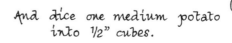

4 Dice one medium carrot.

And dice one medium potato into ½" cubes.

150

5 Add diced vegetables & ½ cup frozen peas to the lentils & rice.

Reduce heat to simmer.

The next step is my own embellishment to Baba's original recipe: the addition of a TARKA—an aromatic fried spice mixture which gives this khichuri some extra zing.

Heat 1 Tbsp mustard oil in a small pan. When the oil is hot, add ½ tsp mustard seeds, ½ tsp nigella seeds & ½ tsp cumin seeds. Once the mustard seeds start to pop, add:

1 small onion, sliced thinly.

2 cloves of garlic, minced.

1-2 small green chilies, sliced. (Optional)

Sauté until onion is nicely browned.

AND **THEN** add

1 small tomato, sliced.

And cook until reduced.

6 The khichuri's done when all the water's been absorbed. At which point, add the tarka and mix.

Garnish with chopped cilantro.

And serve with wedges of lime.

Yum! Perfect on a rainy Sunday.

Play some Rabindra Sangeet* for an authentic Bengali experience!

Needs more ginger.

BABA!

Just kidding, beti!

* OLD BENGALI SONGS WRITTEN BY RABINDRANATH TAGORE.

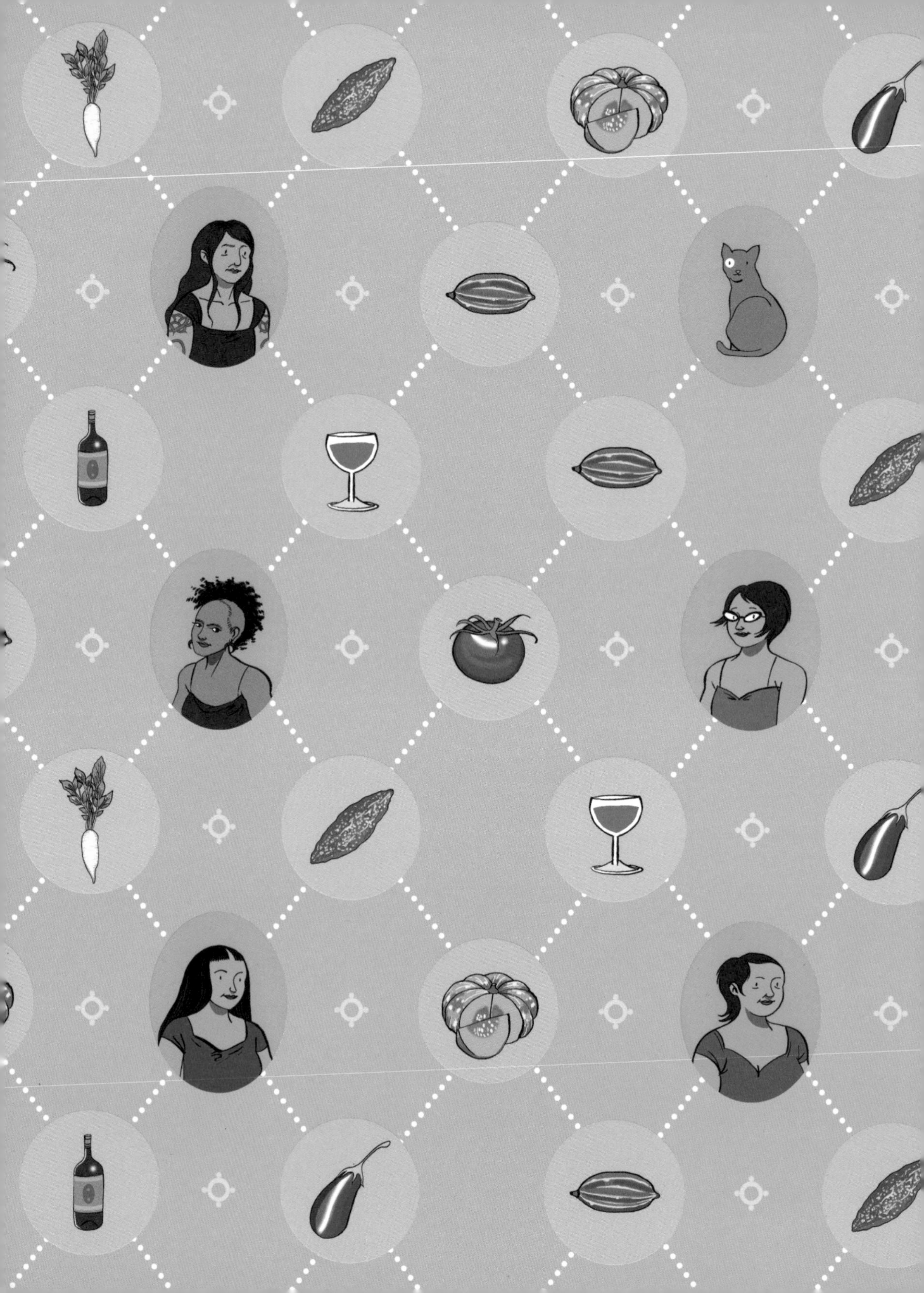